THE BOOK OF
REINCARNATION
AND
THE AFTERLIFE

CHINESE POPULAR CLASSICS

This new and innovative Chinese Popular Classics series will take you to the heart of the Chinese world. One quarter of the world's population is Chinese, yet the great and ancient culture of China is barely known in the West. This is especially true of the popular beliefs which have shaped folk religion and culture in China for over 2000 years. These beliefs offer insights and understanding of relevance for the wider world and are increasingly being recognised as significant religious and spiritual teachings. What was in the past often dismissed by the scornful West as superstition or peasant lore, is now seen to reflect centuries of wisdom.

The team behind the series comes from the International Consultancy on Religion, Education and Culture (ICOREC) who for over twelve years have led the way in translating Chinese religious texts. It is headed by Martin Palmer, whose translations of Chinese texts have established him as one of the foremost interpreters of Chinese religion in the UK today. The team brings together Taoist priests, monks, organisations such as the China Taoist Association, feng shui masters, scholars of classical Chinese, poets and researchers, both in the UK and China. With their assistance it is possible to explore the mythological and philosophical, practical and mystical worlds of popular Chinese culture.

To understand China you need to understand her soul. Through this series, such a journey of exploration can begin.

CHINESE
POPULAR CLASSICS

THE BOOK OF

REINCARNATION

AND

THE AFTERLIFE

MARTIN PALMER
& JOANNE O'BRIEN

SERIES EDITOR

MARTIN PALMER

PIATKUS

Acknowledgements

We would like to thank all our friends and colleagues in the UK, Hong Kong, Macau and China who have made this book possible.

The cover embroidery is a detail of a red silk brocade panel from the Ming Dynasty, 1368–1644. The panel is woven with a delicate pattern of swallows in flight amongst flowering prunus branches. The birds are worked in gilded paper. Both the swallows and prunus flowers are emblematic of spring. The panel is reproduced courtesy of Spink and Son Ltd, London.

First published in 1996 by
Judy Piatkus (Publishers) Ltd
5 Windmill Street, London W1P 1HF

A catalogue record for this book is
available from the British Library

ISBN 0-7499-1602-8

Designed by Chris Warner
Chinese woodcuts © Circa Photo Library

Set in 10.5/12pt Sabon by
Action Typesetting Ltd, Gloucester

Printed and bound in Great Britain by
Biddles Ltd, Guildford & King's Lynn

CONTENTS

INTRODUCTION

What happens at death? Do you become a spirit, reside in a heavenly land, become immortal, or be reborn in a physical body. All these are possibilities in Chinese traditional religion. The dominant belief in most cultures is usually more specific. For example, all the Abrahamic faiths, Judaism, Christianity and Islam believe in one life followed by an afterlife of various kinds. Buddhism, Hinduism and Sikhism, however, believe in many lives and thus in reincarnation. Yet here is a book claiming to cover both.

Chinese traditional religion is unusual in that it has developed a unique synthesis and co-existence of faiths which means that an ordinary Chinese person feels quite at liberty to hold at the same time what to others seem mutually exclusive views.

Reincarnation first came to China as one of the core teachings of Buddhism, when it began to infiltrate the Celestial Kingdom in the first century AD. It encountered a world of vague teachings about the afterlife which already incorporated beliefs that the dead both became ancestral spirits and vengeful demons. To many, reincarnation offered a more logical and ordered understanding of what happens at death. Yet reincarnation has never replaced belief in ancestors nor in baleful spirits which haunt the physical world. It is the particular genius of China that this situation, which in many other cultures could have led to warfare and bloodshed, has actually created a culture which knows how to live with this diversity of views.

Reincarnation has risen in popularity in the West in recent decades. Partly this is due to the decline of traditional Christianity's hold over people's imagination, partly due to the increased numbers of Buddhists and Hindus active in the West, but also partly due to a search for a greater sense of belonging to something greater. In the search for a meaning to life and a cause for suffering, the belief in reincarnation has come to lodge firmly alongside more traditional Western views of what happens to us after death.

Some people look to reincarnation to provide a set of guidelines by which life can be lived. This was taken a step further in China and specific tables were drawn up to spell out the cause and effect of certain actions (see pp. 15–17). But reincarnation cannot be summed up as a set of rules. It is about finding meaning and purpose for life now and of putting this present life into a wider, longer term perspective. If one believes that this is but one life amongst many, then the pressure to 'succeed' – whatever that might mean – in this life, is eased. I have a friend who believes in reincarnation and who has decided that in this life he will not marry. He has decided this because he wishes to concentrate on spiritual aspects of himself this life, but he looks forward to the joys of sex and marriage, family and children in the next life. It is this perspective which many find so attractive about reincarnation.

Yet we would be foolish to believe that we can simply adopt a system of belief without bringing to it all sorts of ideas and notions inherited from our own historic traditions. This is why the Chinese model is so important. For it shows us how a pluralist culture can exist in which diversity of views complement each other rather than divide. In looking into the worlds of different beliefs about what happens at death in traditional Chinese teachings, we can glimpse a new way of exploring and balancing both the old and the new in our own cultures and lives.

THE MEANING OF LIFE AND DEATH - THE CHINESE TAO

THE DIVERSITY OF DESTINY

BY THE GREAT CENTRAL LAKE in the picturesque city of Hangzhou on the coast of China stands a tomb. It contains the beheaded body of Yue Fei, a famous general who was executed for treachery in 1142. Yet within a few decades this disgraced soldier was being worshipped as the city's god, to whom petitions and prayers were brought to avert plagues, siege

1

or economic collapse. Soon stories were beginning to circulate that he was none other than the reincarnated phoenix which stands on perpetual guard by the side of the Buddha, ready to strike down any who would do him harm. Under the Communists, Yue Fei has been elevated to the status of a patriotic hero and worshipped for his selflessness in the face of the enemy and his cry: 'Return our mountains and rivers.'

How, you may be wondering, is it possible for one person to be a city god, a dead human being, a reincarnated phoenix of the Buddha and a Communist folk role model – not to mention a traitor who becomes a hero? Welcome to the world of Chinese beliefs about life both before and after death.

Chinese attitudes to life and death are shaped by Taoism, Confucianism and Buddhism. Whereas in the West we expect people to adhere to one set of teachings or another, Chinese religion makes use of all three, often at the same time, and may add a splash of Christianity or a dash of Hindu ideas just for fun. The different versions of the Yue Fei story illustrate these three main strands perfectly.

The Confucian Version

Yue Fei was born in 1103 under the weak rule of the emperors of the Southern Song, so called because they had lost the north of China to invading tribes. Nevertheless Yue Fei, as a good Confucian, was loyal to the dynasty. He was also loyal to his mother and to the virtues she impressed upon him – literally so, for when he joined the army she tattooed the words 'Loyal even unto death for my country' upon his back.

Over the years he rose in authority. In 1140, now a general, he led a vast peasant army north and counter-attacked the invading Mongolians, inflicting a crushing defeat. He was all for pressing on to recapture more of northern China, but was betrayed. Back in Hangzhou the prime minister Qin Hui and his wife were in contact with the enemy. They had no love of China itself, and saw in Yue Fei a potentially strong new emperor who would foil their own plans to rule.

This couple and two fellow conspirators poisoned the mind of the current feeble Emperor and made him summon the general home, where the evil minister accused him of treachery and of planning to usurp the throne. Yue Fei denied the charges and removed his shirt to reveal the words of loyalty tattooed upon his back, but to no avail: the gullible Emperor consented to the execution of the general and his son.

Meanwhile, the treacherous faction arranged a treaty which handed over most of China to the invaders. Many years later, when the Chinese reasserted themselves, this betrayal was reviled and Yue Fei honoured. A temple was built beside his tomb in 1221 and he was praised by poets and statesmen, who extolled him as a model Confucian scholar-warrior. Even in the twentieth century the Communists present him as a great patriotic general.

The Taoist Version

So at one level Yue Fei is venerated as a noble ancestor who exemplifies the true virtues of a Confucian – filial piety and loyalty. The Taoist version follows much the same course, except that in his fight against the invaders Yue Fei has the assistance of various Taoist gods and magicians who fight the evil spirits which accompany the enemy hordes. Yue Fei becomes a fighter against evil in this world and in that of the spirits. His success is the victory of good over evil; his betrayal is the cost of such a struggle, for from his example comes the power to fight back.

But it is after his death that he really comes into his own. By popular acclaim, later confirmed by the ruling emperors, Yue Fei was worshipped as the city god of Hangzhou. This meant that he was believed to dwell now in Heaven, in the court of the Taoist ruler of Heaven, the Jade Emperor. There, along with the gods of the other cities of China, he cared for his city, ensuring that the prayers and entreaties of the faithful were heard and disasters avoided or mitigated. The temple surrounding his tomb was enlarged to make space for the hundreds of worshippers who brought their tribulations to him and offered him food, incense and devotion. Yue Fei had become a god.

The Buddhist Version

Once upon a time the Buddha was meditating, protected by the phoenix, who never sleeps but guards him night and day. Into the room flew a strange and noisy spirit of discord known as the old white bat. It disturbed the meditations of the Buddha and, to protect him, the phoenix leaped upon the intruder and tore it to pieces.

But Buddha was angered by the over-zealous action of the phoenix and, to punish him, sent him to be reborn upon Earth in the form of a white eagle. This was a most demanding incarnation within which to work for salvation from his previous action, for the eagle is itself a violent creature which lives by killing. Nevertheless the phoenix sought to control his instincts in the hope of rebirth in a more favourable form. Sadly, this was to no avail. One day he spied a tortoise on a river bank. Overcome with the desire to kill he swept down, seized the poor creature and devoured it.

Through the cycle of rebirth the Buddha decided to provide another opportunity for his faithful servant to redeem himself. So the phoenix/white eagle was reborn as Yue Fei, the brave and patriotic general. Despite his valiant defence of his country and his unassailable loyalty he was betrayed by the Emperor's adviser Qin Hui, who was none other than the poor tortoise which the phoenix had killed in his previous life, and Qin Hui's even more treacherous wife, who was the reborn spirit of the old white bat. The tortoise and the old white bat, intent on revenge, told the Emperor that Yue Fei was conspiring with the enemy. In fact, they themselves were the traitors.

The phoenix, in the form of Yue Fei, proved to have learned his lesson. Despite terrible provocation he remained loyal to his oath of obedience. He could have summoned his army and overthrown the Emperor, but he did not. He could have attacked Qin Hui and his wife, but he did not. He could have fled to safety, but he did not. He took the punishment imposed on him, always protesting his total loyalty and showing that on his own back his mother had tattooed: 'Loyal even unto death for my country.'

After his execution he had to undergo the most awful punishments in the eighteen Buddhist Hells before his countrymen recognised his real virtue and erected a temple over his tomb. When this happened, the Buddha was able to send a message to the Judges of Hell demanding that the soul of Yue Fei, the phoenix, be released and be given back its phoenix form. The phoenix who never sleeps continues to guard the Lord Buddha day and night.

But Qin Hui and his wife had fallen prey to vengeance and violence. For them the cycle of dreadful rebirths has only just begun; they will turn in suffering for eighty thousand rebirths, each one as dreadful as the next, until they have cleansed themselves of the crime against Yue Fei.

If you visit the tomb and temple of Yue Fei in Hangzhou today what will probably strike you most of all are the statues. In front of his tomb stand four iron statues, representing the four conspirators who plotted his death. In China, statues are normally carved from stone. But stone is permanent and therefore reserved for the good. These four traitors have souls in torment and their statues are made from iron, which can be melted down and recast – a symbol of their numerous rebirths and the state of their souls.

The key to understanding Chinese beliefs about life after death, and especially reincarnation, is the knowledge that in Chinese philosophy we have more than one soul. Indeed we have ten souls, three of one type and seven of another.

THE TWO TYPES OF SOUL

In common Chinese belief, each person has two types of soul. At death one remains with the body and is the ancestor spirit, while the other descends to the Hells to be punished until ready to be reborn. In ancestor worship it is the first kind of soul, the one which joins the family of the dead and watches over the living family, which is more important. We shall explore what happens to the second in its travails in the Hells in Chapter 5.

The two kinds of soul have different names. The first is called the po and is yin (see p. 10) in nature, linked indissolubly with the Earth to which it returns at death and from where it watches over the family. It is this soul which is the ancestor spirit, worshipped both at the tomb and in the home through the ancestor tablet. The other soul is known as the hun and is yang in nature. This is the soul which travels to the Hells, where it is purged and then reborn. The po is known as the terrestrial soul, of which there are seven varieties, while the hun is the celestial soul, of which there are three varieties.

The notion of two kinds of soul appears in Taoist literature from at least the fourth century AD, for example in the early fourth-century *Pao Pu Tzu (Master of Preservation of Existence)*, and obviously dealt with an emerging problem. The earliest understanding of what happened to the soul after death was that it became an ancestor spirit and was worshipped in this form. When Buddhism began to take hold in China in the first three centuries AD it introduced the notion of recincarnation, adding to the religious mix of Shamanism, Taoism and Confucianism. By the fifth or sixth century the new religion was rising rapidly in popularity and reincarnation was widely accepted. The dilemma was how to square this with ancestor worship. The answer was complex and depended upon the hun/po theory, as will be explored in Chapter 4.

A bigger problem confronted Taoism. It was originally rather vague about the afterlife but, under pressure from popular interest in Buddhist concepts of reincarnation, Taoism had to offer something. It took a theme from its past, immortality, and developed extensive systems related to this theme (see Chapter 3). It also took some of the elements of Buddhist teachings on reincarnation and incorporated them into its own system. This is why Taoists also have Hells and rebirth, though their explanations of how and why rebirth takes place are still a little vague!

In popular belief, the three key belief systems – Confucianism, Taoism and Buddhism – are not seen to be in opposition. This is made clear in the *Three Lives Book*, a fascinating work compiled in the fifteenth and sixteenth centuries and used by traditional families at the birth of a son. This book was used to calculate an individual's fortune in past, present and future lives (see Chapter 8). It combines all three systems almost effortlessly. Before we go further, let's take a look at them in some detail.

CONFUCIANISM

Named after Kung Fu Tzu (Latinised as Confucius), a wise teacher who lived in the fifth century BC, in Chinese Confucianism is known as Kung Chiao – the teachings of Kung. Confucius or Kung was born in 551 BC and died, apparently a failure, in 479 BC. During his lifetime, his advice on how to run a state was largely ignored, even though he was actually employed as an adviser. His core teaching was based on the ancient past, when China had been ruled by emperors who followed the Tao or Way of Heaven by acting morally and ethically and by conducting the correct rituals. He constantly urged a return to old values to counteract the corrupting influence of modern times. Central to all this was a belief in the importance of a benevolent hierarchy. This is summed up by filial respect from a son to his father, rising up to the loyalty of the subject for the Emperor. Kung believed that if everybody had a place and felt secure within it, society would run smoothly. But this depended upon each person in the chain being benevolent to those below them and obedient to those above.

The role of women was always to be subservient to all men, which explains something about modern Chinese society which the West often finds incomprehensible. In all its imperial history, since 221 BC, China only ever had one empress who ruled in her own right – the Empress Wu, who was on the throne from AD 690 to 705. Women have never officially counted. This is why, even to this day, girl babies run the risk of being killed at birth: they are often simply not wanted. Sons are all-important. Hence the Chinese saying: 'The three great misfortunes of life are when young to bury one's father; in middle age to lose one's wife; in old age to have no sons.'

The teachings of Kung were collected by his disciples and published, not long after his death, in a book known as *The Analects*. A century or so later the value of his teachings was recognised and they were elevated almost to the status of a religion. Right down to the present, Confucian values have remained the hallmark of Chinese society.

A Continuing Influence

There are two major ways in which Kung's teachings have shaped and influenced China down the centuries. The first is the whole apparatus of Chinese rule, administration and official scholarship, which remained virtually untouched from the second century BC to the early twentieth century. Indeed, the way China is ruled and organised today, under the Communists, owes a great deal to Confucian models.

The famous examination system of Imperial China used only the Confucian classics as the basis of education, for it was held that the answer to any problem could be found by studying them.

The codes of behaviour which underpinned Chinese bureaucracy, while often flouted, were nevertheless strict and highly ethical. For example, the idea that anyone with a grievance could petition the Emperor, even if the grievance was due to an action of the Emperor's, was a reflection of Kung's philosophy of loyalty and benevolence.

The second way in which Confucian ideas have shaped China is via the family and through rituals and beliefs about death. Filial piety, respect and reverence for parents, grandparents and ancestors, is still an essential aspect of Chinese life as it has been for over two thousand years. One of the mythological founding emperors of China, Shun, is supposed to have been chosen by his predecessor precisely because of his filial piety. His father, stepmother and stepbrother hated him and tried to kill him on various occasions, but he survived and never ceased to show his parents due respect and honour. Eventually they repented of their evil ways and became models of righteousness themselves.

In terms of death rites, a son has a vital role to play. Only a son can make the appropriate sacrifices, attend the rituals and ensure that his father's body is buried in a suitable site in accordance with the rules of feng shui (see p. 25). Kung is recorded in *The Analects* as emphasising this point: 'Parents, when alive, should be served with propriety; when dead should be buried according to propriety.'

It is at this level – veneration and fear of one's ancestors – that Confucianism retains its strongest hold on Chinese popular culture. Confucian teaching holds that the dead are still 'living' members of the family. Indeed, while no longer physically present – except for their tablet on the family shrine – they exert even more power than when alive. Offend an ancestor and he or she might blight your career, ruin your marriage or bring illness upon you. Respect your ancestors and all should go well for you.

As a result, the ancestors are never ignored by the Chinese. Offered food and incense every day, they are especially cared for at major festivals such as Chinese New Year and in particular at the ancestor festival of Ching Ming in late spring (see Chapter 7). At this festival, families go out *en masse* to clean their ancestors' tombs and to celebrate with them in the graveyards by offering food such as whole roast pigs.

TAOISM

The word 'Tao' originally meant just a road or path, a use it retains to this day. But from around the seventh century BC it also began to have a more spiritual significance, meaning the Way or the Path to be followed. Tao is not a deity or supernatural being: it is simply the Way of Nature, the Way of the Universe. It is how things should be. To follow the Tao is to follow the natural way; not to fight against what comes, but to flow with it. Tao is most beautifully described in the classic *Tao Te Ching*, a text believed to have been compiled in the fourth century BC (see Bibliography).

> *The Tao*
> > *pours out everything into life –*
> *It is a cornucopia*
> > *that never runs dry*
>
> *It is the deep source of everything –*
> > *it is nothing, and yet in everything.*
>
> *It smooths round sharpness*
> *and untangles the knots.*
>
> *It glows like the lamp*
> *that draws the moth ...*
>
> *Tao exists, Tao is*
> *but where it comes from I do not know.*
>
> *It has been shaping things*
> > *from before the First Being,*
> > *from before the Beginning of Time.*

The earliest Taoists were in fact philosopher sages from about the sixth to the third century BC who wrote about the Tao – a term also used extensively by Kung Fu Tzu. But they did not use the term to describe themselves. It was first used in the first or second century AD, in reference to religious practitioners who used Taoist ideas to heal and offer salvation and to organised religious communities, structures and beliefs. This form of Taoism was in fact a fusion between the oldest religion of China, shamanism, and the philosophical insights of the philosophers of the Tao.

Shamanism goes back over five thousand years at least, and from about 1800 BC to about 1000 BC was the dominant religious and social force in China. It posits two worlds: the first the physical world which we all inhabit, the other a spiritual world which is superior. Occasionally the spiritual world, or its inhabitants, break through into our own. A shaman is able, when in a state of trance, to communicate between these two worlds and to negotiate with the spiritual powers for healing or help. With the rise of the Confucians, shamanism was pushed more and more to the edge of Chinese society and regarded as no more than a legacy from a primitive past. However, it re-emerged as part of the practices of Taoism in the first and second centuries AD.

The Pursuit of Immortality

Taoism, as it has developed over the centuries, offers two things. First, it offers a supernatural world which can be invoked to come to the aid of those who are oppressed or in need. For example, the Eight Immortals (see p. 42) exemplify the virtues of helping the downtrodden and the poor overcome their troubles. Secondly, Taoism offers the possibility of living within your own body for ever: the pursuit of immortality, as it is known. This concept is described further in Chapter 4.

This pursuit of immortality, coupled with the fantastic world of deities, is seen at its most vivid with regard to views about life after death. To this day Taoists claim that certain good people or those who practise various rituals and meditational practices have escaped death altogether. But if death does come, the Taoist's concern is to ensure that the deceased is properly buried according to the rules of feng shui and that the proper offerings have been made to assist the dead person through the troubles, trials and horrors of the Ten Taoist Hells (see Chapter 5) and into their next life.

Yin and Yang: an Essential Tension

At the heart of the Taoist vision of life and death is the dynamic tension which exists between yin and yang. These two primordial forces – yin female, cold, wet and earthy; yang male, fiery, dry and heavenly – are locked in perpetual struggle, but can never overcome each other for they both contain the seed of the other. Thus just as summer, which is yang, gives way to autumn, which is yin, so the world and all things within it contain and express the struggle between these two forces. Taoist ritual, prayers and beliefs are concerned with ensuring that the dynamic tension between yin and yang – seen as the main physical manifestations of the Tao – are kept in balance. Humanity's role is to maintain that balance; any action which pushes the world towards a more yin way or a more yang way spells disaster.

Taoists are often pictured as the opponents of Confucianism. For while the Confucians ruled the court and the world of bureaucracy and power, the Taoists withdrew to the quiet of mountains and monasteries. As such they are the world-renouncers who keep the world spinning, for what they renounce is the false world of power and struggle, affirming the true world of the flow of the Tao.

BUDDHISM

It was from the mid-first century AD that Buddhism came into China from India. By the end of the fourth century it had spread widely and was exerting a greater influence over Chinese life than any other external force until the arrival of Marxism in the 1920s.

China took Buddhism and produced its own highly distinctive versions of it. First, it produced major new traditions such as Ch'an Buddhism which, when transferred to Japan in the eighth and ninth centuries AD, became Zen. Secondly, it produced folk Buddhism, with its array of gods and goddesses and its close links to earlier forms of religion such as shamanism, Taoism, and divination. By the sixth century AD monasteries had sprung up all over China, and in terms of formal structures and hierarchies the new religion soon outstripped Taoism.

The Concept of Karma

Buddhism teaches that through the actions of today, tomorrow is shaped. Karma, the accrued effects of past deeds, shapes who you are. As Hui Yuan, the famous fourth-century AD Chinese

Buddhist abbot, said: 'The sutra says that karma has three kinds of response; first, in the present life; second in the next life; and third, in later lives. In the second, the deeds are rewarded in the next life, while in the third, the deeds are rewarded in the second, third, hundredth or thousandth life afterwards.'

The inevitable consequence, for this life and the next, of actions done in the past and today, led to two developments in Chinese Buddhism. The first was the attempt to work out what actions merited what doses of good or bad karma; hence the lists of merit tallies available all over China, which tell you the exact cost of a particular action (see pp. 15–19). By keeping a daily account, many folk Buddhists attempt to control or at least assess the damage they have done and see what gifts – usually to the monks – are necessary to buy their way out of the karmic consequences. One popular text, the *Yin Kuo Ching* (*Classic of Consequence Action*), lists the following actions and their consequences. All are equally applicable to women.

- *Why does this man today hold a high position?* Because in his previous life he paid for the statue of the Buddha to be decorated with gold.

- *Why does this man get to have a fancy car?* Because in his previous life he contributed towards building bridges and repairing roads.

- *Why is he able to dress so well in this life?* Because he donated robes to Buddhist monks in his previous life.

- *Why does he not have to worry about food and clothes?* Because he gave alms to the poor in his previous life.

- *Why is this man so rich he can afford a luxury mansion?* Because in his previous life he took his donation of rice to the door of the convent.

- *Why is he so lucky and prosperous in this life?* Because in his previous life he made generous donations towards the building of a convent and a public pavilion.

- *Why is he so dignified in his appearance?* Because he offered flowers on the altar of the Lord Buddha in his previous life.

- *Why is he so wise?* Because in his previous life he prayed and chanted to the Lord Buddha daily.

- *Why is his marriage so successful?* Because he offered streamers and silk pennants before the altar of the Buddha in his previous life.

- *Why are both his parents still alive?* Because in his previous life he was kind to the lonely.

- *Why does he have so many sons and grandsons?* Because he liberated caged birds in his previous life.

- *Why does he enjoy such a long life?* Because in his previous life he bought livestock and set it free.

- *Why does she become a widow in this life?* Because she scorned her husband in her previous life.

- *Why does he become a slave in this life?* Because he forgot to return favours in his previous life.

- *Why is his eyesight so good in this life?* Because in his previous life he donated money for the oil to light the statue of the Buddha.

- *Why is he deaf and dumb in this life?* Because he was rude to his parents in a past life.

- *Why has he become a cow or a horse in this life?* Because he did not bother to discharge his debts in his previous life.

- *Why is he so healthy in this life?* Because in his previous life he donated medicines for the treatment of the sick.

- *Why is he all alone without relatives or friends in this life?* Because he was evil in his previous life and harmed others.

The second development, or in this case extension of an earlier tradition, was that of the compassionate bodhisattva. A bodhisattva is one who, through countless lives, has built up such a credit of good karma that he could escape the wheel of reincarnation, the endless cycle of life, death and rebirth, if he so desired. But instead of release into Nirvana, the bodhisattva vows to use his immeasurable store of good karma to help rescue those who have done wrong or who have just not managed to build up the karma necessary to escape painful rebirth. The vow of the bodhisattva is most moving:

> A bodhisattva resolves: I take upon myself the burden of all sufferings ... And why? At all costs I must bear the burdens of all beings ... I have vowed to save all beings. All beings I must set free. The whole world of living beings I must rescue, from the terrors of birth, of old age, of sickness, of death and rebirth, of all moral offence, of all states of woe, of the whole cycle of birth–death, of the jungle of false views, of the loss of wholesome dharma ... from all these terrors I must rescue all beings. (Dhamma is the true nature of things, the law of the spiritual path.)

By invoking a bodhisattva such as the goddess of mercy, Kuan Yin, the believer, is thought to be able to achieve forgiveness for his actions and release from the consequences of those actions – if not in full, then at least in part. Given that Chinese Buddhism describes the afterlife, prior to reincarnation, as containing up to eighteen Hells each more dreadful than the one before, any help that can be offered to escape the consequences of your actions is to be welcomed!

FATE: PREDESTINED OR IN YOUR OWN HANDS?

In essence, Chinese tradition teaches that certain things about your life are fated. They are: when you are born; into what kind of family; whether you will start out on a secure financial basis; what sex you are; and whether you are born good-looking. But beyond this your fortune lies in your own hands. If you are a person of depraved tastes and behaviour, you will create one kind of future for yourself. If you are a generous, caring and kind person, you will create another kind of future for yourself. And these can be changed. Thus, if you are an unpleasant, grumpy type who comes to realize that this attitude is destructive to you and your relationships and becomes more open and friendly, then your fortune and fate will change. This concept also affects your next life.

Fate is not fatalistic: this is the heart of Chinese beliefs about life and death. What you do makes you who you are and what you will become. By actions of compassion and kindness you can alter your fate, both in this world and the next. In temples in China it is very common to pick up little booklets which contain a chart on which you can calculate the amount of merit you earn by certain actions. With this chart goes a table showing how many merit points you need to ensure rebirth in a wealthy family, or as a handsome and successful person. But the reverse is also true. Evil or selfish actions can wipe out your merits and face you with the risk of being punished later on in this life or in the next. The following extracts are adaptations of material in the *Yin Kuo Ching*.

Merit Charts
Cause: Making donations to decorate the statue of the Buddha. *Consequence:* To be rewarded with a noble title or high-ranking government office.
Cause: Making offerings of fresh flowers to honour the Buddha. *Consequence:* To become beautiful and attractive.
Cause: Alms-giving in the form of giving away garments and cloth. *Consequence:* To become rich enough to dress in silk and satin.
Cause: Offering rice to the monastery for monks or nuns. *Consequences:* To become rich enough to live in luxury mansions.
Cause: Helping the weak and giving alms to the poor. *Consequence:* To be able to dress in purple silk robes.
Cause: Abstaining from killing domestic animals and setting them free. *Consequence:* To be rewarded with many offspring.

Cause: Making donations to build bridges and roads for public use.
Consequence: To travel in private vehicles.

Cause: Respecting the aged and the wise and virtuous.
Consequence: Reward combining luck, wisdom and long life.

Cause: Helping others with the solution to problems.
Consequence: To be loved by everybody.

Cause: Performing many good deeds for everybody.
Consequence: To have a wife and daughter-in-law who are beautiful and virtuous.

Cause: Feeling hatred for other people.
Consequence: To be unable to bring up one's own son.

Cause: Violating another's wife and daughter.
Consequence: To remain a bachelor for life.

Cause: Frequent reading of obscene books.
Consequence: Blindness.

Cause: To stir up trouble among other people.
Consequence: Frequent bleeding.

Cause: Not believing when hearing Buddhist doctrine.
Consequence: To become deaf in both ears.

Cause: Ill treatment of domestic animals.
Consequence: The whole body will be infected with spots and ulcers.

Cause: Jealousy
Consequence: To develop bad body odour.

Cause: Gossiping frequently.
Consequence: Mis-shapen mouth at birth.

Cause: Beating one's parents.
Consequence: To develop a deformed hand.

Cause: Demolishing a road or a bridge.
Consequence: Both feet will be crooked.

Cause: Gloating at others' misfortunes.   *Consequence:* Permanent ill health.
Cause: Being deliberately misleading.   *Consequence:* To become a pig or dog in the next life.
Cause: Refusing to rescue others in danger.   *Consequence:* Imprisonment.
Cause: Harming others by spreading rumours.   *Consequence:* To die as a result of poisoning by others.
Cause: Looking down on servants.   *Consequence:* To be short and ugly in appearance.
Cause: Benefiting oneself by harming others.   *Consequence:* To commit suicide by hanging.
Cause: Slandering monks or nuns.   *Consequence:* To be hit by thunder or burned by fire.
Cause: Inciting hatred in others.   *Consequence:* To be bitten by a tiger or snake.
Cause: Jeering at beggars.   *Consequence:* To starve to death at the roadside.
Cause: Not loving one's wife and children.   *Consequence:* To be widowed and lonely.

To recap, fate is largely in your own hands; through actions, you can earn merit which will ensure that both in this life and in the next you can improve your position. But that said, no one leads a blameless life. There are sins and crimes, selfish actions and thoughtless deeds for which atonement is required. What happens at death to deal with all this accumulated bad baggage?

Three things happen, because there are the three faiths. Confucianism teaches your descendents, especially your son, to pray for you and to make offerings to you for your comfort in the next life. Good prayers mean the end of bad consequences. Taoism says your descendants must ensure that you are buried in an auspicious place, and that you are accompanied into the after-life by goods which will make life there bearable until you are born again. Buddhism follows a similar line but stresses the

Account of merit	
	Credit
To pay the debts of a father	10
To worship at a father's burial	50
When rich to marry a deformed girl to whom betrothed when poor	100
To lend an umbrella	1
To build bridges, repair roads, open canals and dig wells: for every four shillings expended	10
To furnish a coffin for the poor	30
To bury a man who has no son	50
To entreat a mother not to commit infanticide	30
To save a child from infanticide	50
To save one hundred insects	1
To bury a bird	1
To turn animals loose, for every fivepence expended	1
To pick up one grain of rice	1
To return what you pick up on the street; for every value of fivepence	1
To give fivepence to beggars	1
For one year not to eat beef or dog meat	5
To publish part of the Classics	100
To forgive a debt	100
To destroy the sterotype plates of immoral books	300
Purity through life	1000

Account of transgressions

	Debit
To love a wife more than father and mother	100
To listen to a wife against one's own brothers	10
To allow a stepmother to ill-treat a first wife's children; each day	1
To be double-tongued	30
To be insincere	10
To have one bad thought	10
To see immoral theatricals	10
To dig up a worm in winter	1
To laugh at an ugly person	3
To soil the page of a book	5
To take meat and wine to a temple	5
To get drunk	5
To be guilty of usury	100
To counterfeit silver	100
To misuse written or printed paper	50
To cook beef or dog meat	100
To dig up a coffin	100
For a mandarin not to prohibit infanticide	10
To assist in infanticide	50
To drown an infant	100
To publish an obscene book	measureless

necessity of good behaviour in this life, to avoid a painful time in the Hells and a bad rebirth. Buddhism alone emphasizes that life after death – reincarnation – is governed almost entirely by the moral quality of this life. What both Taoism and Buddhism also offer is a vision of Hell, or rather Hells, which is enough to make your blood curdle. But you must pass through them in order to be purified enough to be reborn.

Such terrible visions of the afterlife are perhaps a sign of how seriously Chinese tradition takes the notion that what we make of our lives depends upon ourselves. For in the end, Chinese belief says, you are what you make yourself. Be good and you will have good done to you. Be bad, and you will suffer – if not in this life, then afterwards. But this is always tempered by another tradition which says that if you are good to those who have gone before they will be good to you; be good to those who come after you, and they will care for you. You are urged, in other words, to be both a creative individual and a good, filial member of the wider family. And it is to the family and ancestors that we now turn.

2

ANCESTOR WORSHIP

THE ANCESTORS IN EARLY CHINA

To serve the dead as though they were living. To serve the departed as though they were still in our midst. This is the height of filial piety.

Doctrine of the Mean

Perform with care the funeral rites of the recently departed and the sacrifice ceremonies for the long departed ancestors, and as a result the virtue of the people will once again shine forth.

The Analects

21

THIS IS HOW Kung Fu Tzu (Confucius) expresses the importance of ancestor worship for him and for his vision of society. It is what is expected of us if we are to be filial; and by adhering to such values and showing respect in this way, the whole of society benefits. There was no concept of reincarnation in Chinese thought until the coming of Buddhism. Taoist and Confucian thought saw any life after death as either existence in a vague, shadowy underworld about which no details were known, and/or existence as an ancestor.

But what exactly is ancestor worship and why did it become so powerful in Chinese culture? To understand this we need to go back to the earliest history of China, to the dimly perceivable days of the Shang dynasty (c1750–1122 BC) and the better-lit world of the Chou dynasty (1122–770 BC). Ancestor worship lay at the very heart of these early societies. Indeed, according to certain authorities the earliest cities of China had at their centres ancestral shrines and tombs around which the city grew and towards which it was orientated, with the main roads leading into the compound of the shrine.

Oracles: the Origins of Chinese Writing

The reason for this is that the authority and identity of the differing tribes and communities in China were inherently bound up with their own particular ancestors. These ancestors were believed to be able to communicate between the physical world of Earth and the spiritual world of Heaven – the two worlds of shamanism (see pp. 9–10). The ancestors were revered and indeed feared as intercessors between the two worlds. They were, therefore, often asked for help or advice, according to the oracle bones of the Shang dynasty. These remarkable records are the origin of Chinese writing. Shamans would hammer dents into the underside of tortoise shells or ox shoulder bones, ask a question of the ancestor or deity, and then apply a heated stick to the dents. The heat caused cracks to appear on the other side. These were then 'read' as pictures, giving an answer to the question. For example, a set of wavy cracks would be interpreted as a river, and a crack with smaller leg-like cracks running out from its base would be interpreted as a person. If the answer proved to be true and/or auspicious, the 'pictures' perceived in the cracks were etched on more clearly, and this is the origin of Chinese characters.

Honour Your Enemies' Ancestors

All the earliest histories of China stress the vital importance of having the blessing of the ancestors. Once a ruler, or even worse a dynasty, lost this blessing, and with it the support of Heaven, they were bound to fall. When the Chou tribes rose up in rebellion against the Shang dynasty and its tyrannical last emperor, they soon conquered the whole kingdom. As his capital fell to the invaders the last emperor threw himself into a fire and was killed. However, the Chou were very anxious to make sure that some members of the Shang ruling family survived. Why? Because they were then given responsibility and funding, in perpetuity, to maintain the sacrifices to the Shang dynasty ancestors. To take over a corrupt kingdom from a venal ruler was one thing. To insult the ancestors and thus run the risk of retribution from the honourable ancestors of that same dynasty and ruler was quite another. Ancestors could cause serious trouble when upset, even if they were not your own! The Chou also returned every year to their own ancestor temple to offer sacrifices and to give thanks for their victory over the Shang. Two sets of ancestors had to be placated.

One Family, Living or Dead

It is impossible to tell when ancestor worship first became a feature of Chinese society. The surviving oracle bones, myths, legends and fragments in the ancient classics go back to around 1800 BC. However, it would appear that ancestor worship was well entrenched by then, so its roots may lie even further back. Whatever the truth, the central role and power of the ancestors long pre-dates the moralising of Confucius or the establishment of the elaborate Confucian rituals. It is more raw and primitive than that – it is the sense that the dead are still part of the living family, or, perhaps even more truthfully, that the living are but part of the family of the dead.

During the Shang and Chou dynasties only the ruling family and its ancestors were worshipped; most of society was in feudal slavery to the rulers and thus considered of no significance.

However, partly through the Hundred Schools of philosophy, which flourished between the sixth and third centuries BC, partly through the greater integration of China and partly through the ordinary people's growing desire for some element of personal salvation, the theological focus shifted: people now wanted to take part in rituals for themselves. The rise of widespread ancestor worship seems to date from the same period as the rise of many other traditions which stressed personal salvation and participation in the mysteries of Heaven. For example, many of the most common divination methods – physiognomy, horoscopes and feng shui (see opposite) – start appearing around this time, between the third century BC and the second century AD.

ANCESTOR WORSHIP ACCORDING TO CONFUCIUS

Under Confucian teachings, the health and wellbeing of the empire relied on the emperor revering his ancestors and doing that which was dutiful and pleasing to them. This model of obedience continued downwards from emperor to subjects, from father to son, establishing a pyramid of loyalty with the ancestors firmly seated at the top, along with Heaven itself. To ignore or disregard the ancestors was considered the worst possible crime. Respect for the dead meant that not only did you have their names recorded in your ancestral temple in your home village, but every tomb was treated as sacred and had to be – indeed still has to be today – put in a place specially chosen to ensure good fortune.

To this day, as you travel for example from the airport of Xian to the city proper, built on the site of the ancient capital of many dynasties of China, you pass hundreds of vast burial mounds, many of them going back well over two thousand years. They have not been flattened or dug up, for they are the burial places of ancestors – often ancestors of the various dynasties which ruled from here. Over the centuries this has meant that large areas of land have been taken out of normal agricultural use, which is why the Communist government has increasingly encouraged cremation.

What Confucius did in making ancestor worship central to his vision of an orderly society was to build upon a deep tradition which had held sway in China for at least a thousand years before him. His skill lay in turning this clan-based cult into something which buttressed the emperor at the top and placed everyone clearly within a particular stratum of society. Confucius, or to be more precise his followers over the centuries, took a clan practice and turned it into an outward expression of social order and control for a vast empire.

In Chinese folk wisdom there is a saying that only five things remain constant: Heaven, Earth, the noble ruler, one's ancestors and one's teacher. To this day, in traditional Chinese families, Heaven, Earth and the ancestors are worshipped every day. The Earth god has a shrine by the front door, while Heaven and the ancestors have their shrine on the wall or raised upon a special shrine table. The Earth god is the first to be informed of the death of a member of the family and he has a key role in the associated rituals. The veneration of Heaven, Earth and the ancestors is recognised by most scholars as the oldest form of worship practised in China today. The sheer continuity of ancestor worship is a matter of some astonishment, but what does it really mean and what happens?

THE TOMB AND THE ANCESTOR TABLET

In ancestor worship there are two centres of attention, the tomb and the ancestor tablet. The tomb is the most important. Given that the po souls (see p. 5) stay with the physical body, it is essential that the body feels comfortable in its grave and that the burial site should be as auspicious as possible. In other words, the feng shui should be the best possible.

Feng Shui

This is the term for what is often called geomancy in the West. Literally, feng shui means 'wind water' and refers to the forces of nature and our relationship with them. Feng shui stands for a view of the land as being alive with forces with which we need to be in balance in order to avoid disaster. Every place involves a delicate relationship between the two primal forces of yin and yang (see p. 10). Nothing exists but through the dynamic interplay between these two forces, and all living things consist of a balance of these two – for example, the two kinds of souls.

Life is activated by the flow of ch'i – literally 'breath' – which is constantly on the move within us, all living beings and the landscape. Feng shui's skill is to detect the flow of ch'i and the balance of yin and yang in the landscape, and to build in accordance. It has influenced the way the Chinese have built for at least fifteen hundred years, and has given rise to the particular beauty of Chinese landscapes, both rural and urban.

Choosing a burial site

From its earliest days feng shui has been associated with burials. It is clear from the ancient histories that the choosing of an appropriate burial site was vital. The comfort and peace of the dead were of great significance to the living, for an unhappy ancestor could give one a pretty grim present life. The importance of burial for feng shui can be seen in the titles of the two most important books of feng shui, both written in the fourth to fifth centuries AD: *The Burial Classic* and *The Yellow Emperor's Dwelling Classic*. Even today, feng shui masters spend as much time on burial site selection and details as they do on everything else from planning a new office block to altering the family kitchen.

An example of the power and significance of geomancy is given in a well-known story from the seventeenth century. To the north of Chao Ching in Kuangtung province there is a mountain called Seven Star Peak. West of this lies a small hill which looks just like the back of a turtle, and a number of large stones lying in a river at its base look like its head. Turtles in Chinese belief are magical animals, mediums between this physical world and the spiritual world.

Now a rich man had asked a feng shui master to find a good burial site for his ancestors. The feng shui master told him that this turtle hill was the best site around, and especially the area of the turtle's mouth. He said that the turtle had opened its mouth some ten years earlier and was due to do so again, on a date that the master had divined. He suggested to the rich man that on that day he should bury his ancestor there. The rich man agreed and had the coffin of his ancestor dug up ready for the auspicious day.

When the day dawned, the rich man and the feng shui master set out in a small boat bearing the coffin. As they approached the rocks at the base of the hill which formed the turtle's head the river began to swirl, for there was a whirlpool at the mouth of the turtle. As the boat hung precariously on the edge of the whirlpool, the master ordered the rich man and his servants to push the coffin over the side. Without thinking, they did as they were told and the coffin disappeared from sight.

Almost immediately the rich man began to have regrets. This was hardly a conventional place to 'bury' an ancestor, and he was sure bad luck would now afflict him. He was so upset that he took the feng shui master to court, claiming he had been tricked. The judge ordered the feng shui master to return the coffin to the rich man. The master asked to borrow the magistrate's sword, the symbol of his authority and power. Taking the sword, he returned to the site and with one swipe chopped off the top of the stone head, thereby destroying the power of the place. Immediately the coffin bobbed to the surface of the water and was hauled ashore.

The rich man was greatly relieved and opened the coffin to make sure his ancestor's bones were still there. Only then did he realize his mistake, for the site had been auspicious beyond all normal reckoning and his ancestor's bones were now covered with golden scales – a sign of great blessing. But the power of the site was now destroyed, and so he had no option but to bury the coffin in a less auspicious place.

The idea that burial in favourable circumstances increases the wellbeing of a family is touchingly illustrated by the story of Sun Yat-sen's mother's grave. Sun Yat-sen was responsible for the overthrow of the last Imperial dynasty in 1911; he then guided the Chinese Revolution until his death in 1925.

He was born in a humble village near Gwangzhou (formerly Canton) in the south of China and his family was very poor. Yet when his mother died he was the leader of his country. This was taken by the peasants of Gwangzhou as a sign that his mother was blessed by the gods. When she was buried, people began frantically buying up plots of land near her tomb. There they reburied their own parents, believing that being so close to such a blessed and favoured woman, even in death, would rub off on their own ancestors and thus on them.

Finding a really auspicious feng shui site for the burial of your parents or grandparents is the most filial thing that a son or grandson can do. What is important to ancestor worship is that the po soul lies at peace in its last resting place and is visited regularly at the major festivals and especially at Ching Ming, the spring festival devoted to ancestors.

Ancestor Tablets and Temples

The second centre of focus for ancestor worship is ancestor tablets. You will find these in almost all Chinese homes, usually on a special shelf at the back of the main room, lit by a small red light bulb or by candles and accompanied by small trays of fruit and cups of drink and a flower or two in a vase. In many ways this is the centre of the home, and here too will be gathered deities who are particularly dear to the family – a Buddha or two, or Kuan Yin, the goddess of mercy, or Kuan Ti, the god who fights demons.

The tablets vary in size and material from the foot-long painted chipboard of the very poor to the carved chestnut boards of the wealthy. There may be one board or two, but the basic information on them is essentially the same. Painted red, the auspicious colour, a board carries details of the birth date (year, month, day and hour) of the deceased, their name, the date of death (again year, month, day and hour) and the date of burial. The tablet also often tells where the person lived and where they are buried, along with general blessings upon the deceased.

Traditionally, five generations of ancestor tablets are kept in the family shrine. Ancestors before that have their tablets placed in the family clan ancestor temple – usually in the village from which the family originated, sometimes as much as two thousand years ago. It is believed that ancestors further back than five generations are not interested in the present family in the same way, or that their powers have declined so much as to be of little use or threat to the living.

Ancestral temples are impressive places. Dedicated entirely to the dead of the clan, stretching back to the founder figure, they are large halls, usually empty except during great festivals when they heave with visitors, many coming from hundreds or thousands of miles away. They are also a sort of welcoming hall for visitors who are returning to the ancestral area. For example, one colleague of mine can trace his clan family back sixty-eight generations. However, he had never been to his clan village until he was thirty-five. When he went, the first thing that happened was that he was taken to the ancestral temple and there asked to tell the ancestors all about his grandparents, his parents and his own family. They had to have the report before the celebrations could begin!

These temples could be compared to old family homes from which the children have long since departed: dusty, echoing places which are suddenly full of life when the children return, rediscovering treasures from their childhood which they have not taken with them into the wider world. In a very real sense it is the house of the ancestors and, like a house of elderly people, needs the young to bring it alive.

ANCESTOR WORSHIP TODAY

So what does ancestor worship really mean today? Has it held its position over the millennia only to see it disappear in this modern generation? Certainly the Communist Revolution, especially the Cultural Revolution of 1966–75, struck grievous blows against it. The elaborate funerals, the employing of feng shui masters, even the practice of burial have been either banned or heavily curtailed under the Communist regime. Respect for elders as a right was first replaced by the cult of the young and then reversed – but only in favour of ideologically approved elderly people such as Mao Tze Tung. Ancestor halls and temples were singled out for attack and destruction.

But in what has been for some Chinese the increasingly more prosperous atmosphere of the liberalisation of trade and commerce since the 1980s the old clan temples have been amongst the first religious shrines to be rebuilt or repaired, often with overseas Chinese funds. In the countryside, religious burial has appeared again as a common ritual and full funeral services with Taoist or Buddhist priests are becoming much more common. In towns and cities, where land is at a premium, the dead are usually cremated and then their tablets are placed in special ancestor halls attached to Buddhist or Taoist temples, where for a fee the monks and nuns will make the appropriate offerings and prayers.

So perhaps at one level the dead ancestor has become just another serviced sector of society. But at a deeper level the ties of clan, the concepts of loyalty and filial piety and the assumption that one's significance comes from being part of a family rather than an individual are still powerfully at work. Many modern commentators, trying to interpret the sudden and unexpected rise of China, Taiwan, Singapore, Hong Kong and South Korea as major economic and social-political forces, have picked on the Confucian ethic as the basis of their success. Undemocratic, yet not oppressive, Confucian family and state values seem to be working powerfully in favour of a wealthier and more contented Far East than could be imagined by the Far West! The Confucian ethic provides cohesion and stability. It offers extensive family networks both within China and in countries to which the Chinese have emigrated. Many trading agreements are undertaken between states but within just one family, through the connections which clan loyalty provides. Furthermore, the internal loyalty which the family generates is of far greater force than any company loyalty found in the West.

THE VIEW FROM THE WEST

When the Catholic missionaries arrived in China in the late sixteenth century, they found themselves divided over ancestor worship. Some, such as the enlightened Jesuits, argued that there was nothing incompatible between being a Christian and venerating one's parents and ancestors; they pointed to the Ten Commandments and their injunction to honour your mother and father. However, other religious factions felt that anything which smacked of the older culture of China was incompatible with Christianity. In the end, the argument destroyed much of the Church's power in China, for in 1715 the Pope decreed that it was impossible to be a good Christian and also to venerate one's ancestors. The emperor of the time was outraged at this attack upon the very foundation of China and turned from supporting the Church to attacking it; not long afterwards, all but socially useful missionaries were expelled.

This story captures the ambiguity with which ancestor worship is regarded in the West. The notion of respecting one's parents is difficult to accept in the post-Freudian world. Yet at the same time people have begun to look for their roots, to try to understand where they have come from and where they fit into a larger picture than just personal success and gratification. The Chinese relationship with the ancestors is perhaps a timely reminder that we are not just what we make ourselves, but are partly the outcome of our family's past. We can take hold of our lives and shape them to a better end, but we can never ignore what we were born into – a family with relationships, expectations, power struggles, histories and memories. This, at its best, is what ancestor veneration or worship reminds us of, and we forget it at our peril.

3

IMMORTALITY

THE QUEST FOR AN IMPERISHABLE BODY

WHILE BUDDHISTS FOCUSED upon the nature of reincarnation and ways to break the cycle of rebirth, Taoists turned their attention to the search for eternal life. The simple reason is that, unlike adherents of all other religions, the Taoists believed that immortality could only be achieved through a physical body, not despite it. In order to become immortal, they had to transmute the physical body into an imperishable one. In their quest for ways of making the body permanent they consumed dangerous concoctions of poisonous metals and other substances, all imperishable. Ironically, these attempts brought many of them to an early grave but, undeterred by the setbacks, they continued their quest for many centuries.

True immortality, according to Taoism, could only be achieved when the spirit and body were one – the spirit permanently lifted from the suffering of life and death and the body transformed into an eternally healthy vehicle for the spirit. As a result, complex meditational and ritual practices developed to train and purify the mind, while mystifying formulae were drawn up to calculate the amount of mercury, gold or other durable metals needed to preserve the body. When the eternal union of body and spirit had been achieved, then the devout Taoist would be united with the rhythm of Heaven and Earth and with the Tao, and so never die.

SEARCHING FOR THE LANDS OF IMMORTALITY

The idea of longevity going hand in hand with wisdom, success or power has been implanted in the Chinese tradition for more than two thousand years. The earliest myths that speak of the first emperors of China attributed them with healthy long lives of two to three hundred years although none actually achieved immortality. According to the historian Ssu-ma Chien, the desire for immortality was already being expressed by rulers in the fifth century BC. They believed that immortal beings existed in certain remote lands and that, if they could be reached, their secrets would be revealed. By the fourth century BC these lands had been identified as Peng-lai, Fang-hu and Ying-chou, magical islands in the Eastern Sea. Travelling in the opposite direction was the mountain of Kunlun, which was enriched with magical properties; it was believed that immortality would be granted to anyone who reached it. Ssu-ma Chien tells of contemporary rulers sending expeditions in search of this mythical mountain:

Unfortunately, just as the men are about to reach the shores the boats are swept back and away by the wind. In earlier times, some people actually managed to reach them: there the Blessed and the drug that prevents death can be found; there, all things, all birds and the four-footed animals are white and the palaces are made of gold and silver ... There is not one of the rulers who would not have liked to have gone there.

One century later, in 221 BC, the previously warring states of China were united for the first time under Chin Shih Huang Ti, famous today as the Emperor who built the terra-cotta army at Xian. With power and wealth at his fingertips he could pursue one of his abiding interests, the quest for immortality. Familiar with the story of the islands of the Immortals in the Eastern Sea, he built and equipped a fleet to sail in search of them. He filled the ships with thousands of young men and virgins and gave them the blessing, but after they sailed away they were never seen again. Japanese legend however, tells of the arrival of just such a group of people on the shores of Japan and to this day you can visit the shrine raised to their leader.

The Emperor's next plan was to send learned sages and shamans in search of the magic elixir of immortality. These wise men regularly left the palace, but always returned empty-handed. Obsessed with his quest, the Emperor consulted a renowned shaman who, according to Ssu-ma Chien, offered a new suggestion:

Our search for magic fungus, rare herbs and immortals has come to nothing. It seems some sinister influence was against us. It is my sincere opinion that you would be well advised to change your quarters secretly from time to time in order to avoid evil spirits, for in their absence some pure being will come. For subjects to know their sovereign's whereabouts detracts from his divinity. A pure being is one who cannot be wet by water or burned by fire, who rides on the clouds and air and endures as long as heaven and earth.

Inspired by the shaman's words, the Emperor ordered covered walkways to be built to link all his palaces, so that he would never be contaminated by the gaze of onlookers. But his attempt to live for ever failed and he died in 210 BC, eleven years after being declared Emperor of China. His dynasty didn't fare well, either. Although intended to last a thousand years, it collapsed six years later.

The desire to attain immortality did not belong to any particular religion or tradition at this time – it was just an accepted part of Chinese beliefs. But because of Chin Shih Huang Ti's interest traditions were created that were to become the hallmarks of Taoism. By the time Taoism became established in China in the third century AD, the search for immortality was closely linked to its philosophy and rituals.

MYTHS OF IMMORTALITY

However much the ordinary person wished to become immortal, the ways and means of achieving this desired state were in the hands of the powerful, rich or learned. In history and legend the quest is largely the domain of rulers and virtuous sages, and a host of stories were – and still are – related as to how the pill or elixir of immortality was found or given to those worthy of it. One popular legend tells of just such a quest, and to this day it is celebrated every autumn at the Harvest Moon Festival.

At this season, when the brightest moon of the year appears, it is said that a young woman, a rabbit and a tree can be seen in the moon. During her life she was the wife of a cruel and oppressive emperor. He commanded Taoist sages to search the world for the pill of immortality, and eventually they found it in a remote land.

The pill was brought to the palace with great ceremony and the emperor declared that he would swallow it the following day after the necessary ritual had been performed. Word spread quickly amongst his subjects, and fear grew that the country would never be rid of this harsh ruler. The emperor's wife was so concerned for her country and its future that she decided to swallow the pill herself while her husband was asleep. That night she crept into his ante-chamber but, just as she was about to put the pill into her mouth the emperor burst into the room. He rushed towards her, fists raised, as she quickly swallowed the pill. Just as he was about to kill her she began to float above the ground, beyond his reach.

She continued to float towards the heavens until she reached the moon, where the gods protected her.

There are many other stories which focus upon wise men and women who were given the precious gift of immortality and became the heroes of the ordinary people. The most popular stories focus around the Eight Immortals (see p. 42), champions of the poor, ready to exact revenge on the rich or corrupt and quick to remedy injustice. They offered hope to the peasants who had neither the time, education nor money to explore these matters for themselves. The exploits, strengths and foibles of the Immortals were a source of hope and reassurance that justice would be done.

SEEKING IMMORTALITY UNDER COMMUNISM

The quest for immortality has been pursued right up to the present day. Throughout modern China the Eight Immortals are revered and the most powerful ones, such as Lu Tung Pin with his medical skills and Ti Kuai Li, the defender of the poor (see p.43), are worshipped. The Eight Immortals even turn up in major Buddhist shrines, often close to Kuan Yin, the bodhisattva or goddess of mercy. The internal method of achieving immortality, as described below, is followed by many Chinese, from monks on remote mountains to young people in great cities such as Shanghai or Chengdu. Cases are still reported, especially in Taiwan, of people who have achieved immortality, and the prospect of sharing this success is a driving force for many others. This is a tradition which Communism thought it had suppressed. Far from it.

So how does one go about achieving immortality?

HOW TO ACHIEVE IMMORTALITY

When the search for immortality first captured the minds of the ancient rulers they believed that its secret could be found in a pill, in herbs or in an elixir – something that was outside the body. As the belief in immortality developed, so did the range of ways of achieving it. Two schools of thought emerged, each one complementing the other. One concentrated on external methods that required eating, drinking or applying mixtures and lotions which would give the body eternal vigour, while the other focused on internal methods of meditation and mental control over the body which would result in union with the Tao.

The External Method

The search began by looking through the natural world for the most durable metals such as gold and mercury, known to the Chinese as flowing pearl. It was believed that if these could gradually be introduced into the body their qualities would be absorbed, eventually replacing the perishable elements and making the body immortal. Severe illness or fatal poisoning were inevitable but experiments on these metals did lead to early discoveries about the scientific properties of metals.

Minerals such as cinnabar, jade and malachite were also used in the preparation of life-prolonging elixirs. In popular legend the Taoist sage Huang An preserved his body by eating cinnabar, and rested for so many years on the back of a tortoise that the creature's shell became flat. When asked how long he had been resting there, he pointed out that the tortoise fears the light of the sun and moon and only puts its head out of its shell once in every two thousand years. He had seen the tortoise's head emerge five times.

A further, and probably safer, method of prolonging life was the consumption of herbs, flowers, fruit, bark or fungus. All these were believed either to contain vital elements necessary for immortality or to live for a long time themselves, and thus to be capable of assisting longevity. Popular plant substances include the dried root of ginseng, the gum of the peach tree or the charred ash of the mulberry. Some even said that after three hundred years the ginseng plant changed to a man with white blood – the elixir of immortality, a few drops of which would be enough to save a dead man's life. Parts of animals which were associated with long life, such as bats, cranes, deer, turtles and tortoises, were eaten or applied as potions. The tortoise symbolised strength as well as longevity, and it was believed that a preparation made from tortoiseshell could confer a thousand years of life.

As a result of the demand for immortality-inducing materials, many alchemists were preoccupied with making durable precious metals such as gold, and books containing obscure complex formulae were written – but all to no avail. The experiments aimed at making gold were usually funded by the emperor, with the dual prospect of financial gain and immortality. After squandering great sums on alchemical experiments and journeys in search of the Islands of the Immortals, the Emperor Wu (141–87 BC) commented, prefiguring the shift in focus in the search for immortality: 'If we are temperate in our diet and use medicine, we make our illnesses few: this is all that we can attain to.'

Alchemy and other external methods of achieving eternal life seem to have reached their peak in the time of the alchemist Ko Hung, who died in AD 331 at the age of eighty-one. Ko Hung wrote a classic study of Taoist practices called the *Pao Pu*, which is translated as *The Book of the Preservation-of-Solidarity Master*. It combines recipies, concoctions and applications for achieving immortality – a summing up of the many ways of becoming an immortal. Some parts of the book complement each other, while other parts contradict. In amongst the mass of material is a warning to those searching for an easy path to immortality: 'Those who do not carry out acts of virtue and are satisfied only to practise magical procedures will never obtain life eternal.'

After the death of Ko Hung, alchemical experiments went into decline and prominence shifted to the internal transformation of the body.

The Internal Method

The goal of the internal method is to achieve union with the Tao and, although certain external preparations are used, the focus is upon meditation and realisation of the forces at work within the body. At the heart of these life-giving and sustaining forces is ch'i – energy or life breath. Ch'i is channelled throughout the body, where sometimes it is blocked, sometimes it flows too quickly, sometimes it is stagnant and sometimes it is dispersed. The skill lies in recognising and controlling the flow of ch'i, so that the beneficial life breath is not displaced or dispersed. Malign ch'i has to be identified and eradicated, while positive ch'i has to be contained.

This practice emphasises the Embryonic Breath, the original life-giving breath that enters the embryo in the womb. If this original breath can be located and maintained, immortality will ensue. Breathing exercises involve the retention of breath, since in the act of breathing these life-giving forces will be dissipated. Diet is also regulated to control wind, which is why beans, onions and certain grains are excluded from the diet.

Semen – the life-giving force

The second most important life-giving force is semen, which, like the life breath, has to be controlled and contained. (This practice obviously excludes women, but the Taoist tradition is primarily patriarchal and women usually have secondary roles – with the exception of goddesses and Lan Tsai Ho, one of the Eight Immortals.)

It is essential that semen is not wasted, and techniques are developed whereby it is raised but not expelled from the body. One of the ways of internally recycling semen is to withdraw from intercourse just before ejaculation and to squeeze the penis in a way that pushes the semen back into the body to renew the life energy. Numerous texts have been written on the sexual positions which can achieve this state, although many of these works were suppressed by mainstream Taoists who regarded them inappropriate ways of achieving union with the Tao. This method has always been discouraged amongst monks although it was, and to a certain extent still is, practised by interested laymen.

The ideal of these internal life-preserving methods is the fusion of the semen with the Embryonic Breath to create an embryo in the old body which will gestate and then form an immortal body when the old one dies.

Toning the body

The third means of achieving peace and longevity is through physical exercises intended to maintain inner equilibrium. The body is perceived to be a complex world of forces, shifting and reacting, complementing or opposing each other. As well as the movement of the life breaths there is the dynamic interaction of yin and yang, the cold and the hot, the gentle and the powerful. Internal gods are also believed to be at work in different parts of the body, as well as three worms whose task it is to destroy the mortal body and ch'i.

A long catalogue of exercises, each with a specific purpose, has been developed down the centuries to overcome the negative forces and re-establish an inner balance. These meditational exercises are still practised by millions of Chinese as a way of calming and relaxing the mind and body.

The arts of Tai Ch'i and Qigong are now quite popular in the West. Through physical and meditational exercises, the body is assisted to help the ch'i flow freely. *Qigong for Health and Vitality* by Michael Tse is an excellent guide to some of the key practices. He builds upon the sort of exercises that millions of people in China practise every day, usually in the open air in parks. Indeed, not just in China: near us in inner city Manchester is a Chinese old people's home, and early in the morning the elderly residents can be seen doing their ch'i exercises on the grassy traffic island near the home!

The essence of these exercises is to get the body toned and relaxed, enabling you to concentrate on guiding the ch'i through and round the body. One way is to imitate the movement of animals, trying to be as natural and flowing in your movements as possible. Try to move like a cat, but not at speed – just very slowly. Or imitate the movements of a bear stretching after hibernation. The basic idea is to feel your whole body as a linked series of muscles, life forces and energy.

In trying to imagine the ch'i circulating, become aware of each part of your body, step by step. Start by placing your hands on your stomach and from there spreading the ch'i outwards to every part of your body. Stretch and feel the energy flowing into each part of your body.

This practice involves more than physical exercises, however. Many people will do them to music, carefully selected to encourage a peaceful frame of mind. Or they will choose a text from some inspiring book, such as the Bible or the *Tao Te Ching*, and, holding this in their minds as a meditational aid, will focus on its deeper meaning while engaged in these exercises. Think of it as a holistic approach to mind, body and spirit.

To inspire and help them create internal harmony, practitioners seek out remote, peaceful environments; the natural habitat for the sage became a mountain refuge. In Chinese the word for immortal is, in fact, made up of two characters representing a man and a mountain. The tradition of retreat in isolated places continues to this day amongst Taoists in China, particularly on the five major sacred mountains as well as on the scores of other mountains with Taoist associations.

IMMORTALITY IN THE TWENTIETH CENTURY

The belief in immortality continues today in the Taoist tradition, although it is more likely to be pursued through healthy diet, exercise and following the essentials of the Internal Method than by means of dangerous concoctions. Emphasis is placed upon the value of life, and the study of Tao includes the study of how to extend one's life. According to a recent statement of core teachings published by the Taoist Association of China:

People can prolong life through meditation and exercise. These exercises include both the moral and physical sides. People should train their will, discard selfishness and the pursuit of fame, do good deeds, and seek to become a model of virtue.

The achievement of immortality is a reward from the gods for practising worthy acts. With a high moral sense and with systematic exercise in accordance with the Taoist method and philosophy of life, people can keep sufficient life essence and energy in their bodies all their lives. The Taoist exercise of achieving immortality has proved very effective in practice. It can keep people younger and in good health. But there is one point which cannot be neglected: a peaceful harmonious natural environment is a very important external condition.

There have been reports of people from both rural and urban

areas of China and Taiwan achieving immortality. These individuals are usually acknowledged in life for their wisdom and piety, and at death they are buried in a coffin according to traditional Taoist funerary rites. As is the custom, the bones are exhumed three years later to be washed and placed in a pot. All that would remain of a mortal body would be bones and disintegrated flesh, but an immortal's body would have completely disappeared to be replaced by a white feather. Another, but rarer, method of identifying immortality is the complete disappearance of a respected individual. The last recorded case was in Taiwan in 1973, when the body of a doctor was reportedly carried direct to Heaven so that the physical body did not die or corrupt.

THE EIGHT IMMORTALS

Stories of these well-known characters have an enduring quality for the Chinese. They first appeared as Immortals in the thirteenth century, although some are linked back to characters from the T'ang dynasty (AD 618–907). History and fiction have blended to form a rich and colourful mythological tradition, the inspiration for storytellers, actors, writers, artists, poets, sculptors, jewellers and craftsmen for hundreds of years. The Immortals themselves are drawn from a cross-section of society and offer something for everyone, fulfilling the secret hopes and dreams of the ordinary person. Some of them are widely worshipped even today. The most popular are Han Chung Li, Lu Tung Pin, Ti Kuai Li, and Chang Kuo Lao. Their personalities and exploits are revealed in myths and legends, they have achieved popularity as indivudals and it is not unusual to find an altar in a temple dedicated to one of them. When the remaining four Immortals appear it is usually alongside these popular four and when they are mentioned it is frequently as part of a group.

Han Chung Li

Regarded as the founder of the Immortals, Han Chung Li, usually depicted as a plump and scantily clad old man, began adult life as a soldier but was converted to the Tao by an elderly sage. Inspired by these teachings, he abandoned his career and became a mendicant. He is recognised as an alchemist, able to transmute base metal into silver, which he did on one occasion to help the poor buy food in a time of famine. It is said that one day while he was meditating the wall before him cracked open, to reveal a jade casket which contained the secret of immortality.

Han Chung Li's symbols are a feather fan to control the sea, and the peach of immortality which will confer eternal life on whoever consumes it.

Lu Tung Pin

One of the most popular Immortals, Lu Tung Pin followed in his father's footsteps as a state official; but one evening he had a fearful dream of attaining office in the Imperial court, then falling from favour and being cast out as an exile. The shock led him to reject official life and become a Taoist. His commitment was tested many times by demons and physical temptations, but he did not stray.

Lu Ting Pin has strong associations with alchemy and medicine. He knows the formula for the elixir of life and his potions and charms can heal the sick. His temples, dotted on sacred mountains, are popular places of pilgrimage and his shrines in town and village temples are much visited by infirm people. Those praying for recovery can buy charms which are burned before the shrine and the ashes added to water which is kept close to his statue. The water is then drunk, since it is thought to have magical powers.

This Immortal also wields power over evil spirits, destroying or taming them with his powerful sword Chan-yao Kuai, the Devil-Slayer. He is also the provider of charms which are effective against the wiles and evils of demons.

Lu Tung Pin's main symbol is a fly whisk, a traditional sign of someone who can fly at will.

Ti Kuai Li

This crippled and often bad-tempered man is known for his eccentric behaviour as he wanders the country leaning on his iron crutch. He is associated with medicine, and his crutch was often

seen outside apothecaries' shops. He has a history of unpre-
dictability and, although he holds the key to medicinal remedies,
many people would rather consult Lu Tung Pin. It is, however,
that very irascible nature and unpredictable behaviour that catch
the popular imagination and in his crippled form he is seen to be
a defender of the poor and the helpless, fighting for justice on
their behalf.

Ti Kuai Li was not always a cross or disfigured man; originally
he was handsome and healthy. Early in his life he lived as a sage
in the mountains and acquired the gift of flight. One day his spirit
rose out of his body to make a distant journey and a disciple was
left to guard the body until he returned. Ti Kuai Li told the disciple to stand guard for seven days and, if he did not return on the
seventh, the disciple was to burn the body. The faithful disciple
sat with the body but on the sixth day he heard news that his
mother was seriously ill. In haste to return home he burned the
body, and when Ti Kuai Li returned on the seventh day his body
was a pile of ashes. Fearful that he would lose immortality
without a physical body he desperately looked around for
another, recently dead and therefore intact body. In a ditch
nearby lay the fresh corpse of a deformed beggar and Ti Kuai Li
had no choice but to enter his body. And so he is destined to be
a crippled beggar, and in this capacity he uses his magic to help
the poor and oppressed.

A magic gourd containing effective medicines hangs from Ti
Kuai Li's belt; at his command the gourd can also change form,
bewildering his opponents, which is why he is favoured by
professional exorcists.

Chang Kuo Lao

This Immortal is usually seen riding backwards on his donkey at
incredible speed across the sky. He can use his gifts to change his
donkey into paper to fold him away for the night, and in the
morning can bring him back to life with a spray of water from
his mouth.

It was through a chance encounter that Chang Kuo Lao was
given the gift of immortality. He was born into a poor but indus-
trious farming family and took their produce to market on a
donkey. One day, tired from the heat and dust, he rested in the
shade of a temple and fell asleep. Awoken by a wonderful aroma,

he went in search of its source. Eventually he came across some strange herbs simmering in a large iron pot and, tempted by their wonderful smell, ate until he was full. He had no idea that he had stumbled across an alchemist's elixir of immortality. He was discovered by the angry alchemist and, in panic, ran to his donkey and jumped on backwards. Before he realised what was happening, both donkey and Immortal were flying through the air.

Chang Kuo Lao is considered a lucky character and is believed to bring good fortune to couples seeking children, particularly baby boys. His symbols are castanets, a drum or a phoenix feather.

Han Hsiang Tzu

A talented poet, musician and alchemist, he died climbing a peach tree to pluck the fruit of immortality and was transfigured into a Taoist priest. Han Hsiang Tzu is a gentle and contented character with a deep love of beauty and solitude. He is in harmony with the way of nature and at his happiest wandering the mountains, playing his flute and communing with nature. His symbols are the alchemist's crucible and a jade flute and he is regarded as the patron of musicians.

Tsao Kuo Chiu

Originally a wealthy and powerful member of the Imperial court, Tsao Kuo Chiu was a dangerous and scheming adversary. He is also a reformed murderer and there seems to be no reason why he deserved immortality except perhaps caprice on the part of the other seven Immortals, who had an empty cave to fill on their mountain and decided to offer him immortality and a place to live. His symbols are an Imperial tablet of recommendation or a pair of castanets.

Ho Hsien Ku

The only female in the group, Ho Ksien Ku was in her teens when she was given a preparation of powdered mica which changed her into a heavenly body. She was given the peach of immortality and thereafter lived on a rainbow made from oyster shells and moonbeams. Recognised for her piety and generosity, she often holds the lotus flower, symbol of openness and wisdom.

Lan Tsai Ho

Sometimes depicted as a young boy and sometimes as a girl, Lan Tsai Ho represents the outsider or the outcast. In his/her mortal life the money that Lan Tsai Ho made as a flautist and singer was given to the poor, leaving little or nothing for his/her own food or accommodation. Lan Tsai Ho is usually portrayed holding a basket containing peaches, pine, bamboo, chrysanthemum, fruit and flowers associated with immortality.

At one level the Chinese quest for immortality is a serious affair, yet at another level it is about making the most of the present. As the Emperor Wu observed over two thousand years ago, it may be enough to live and eat wisely and healthily in order to make the most of life. And even if immortality is achieved, this does not make you either a better or nicer person. Nor does it stop you having to deal with difficulties and rude or unpleasant people. What immortality is about is living with integrity and for the moment, and striving through this to do nothing to destroy the very essence of your being – the best aspects of your personality and your very own body.

The Internal Method contains much wisdom about how to live a balanced and healthy life. It may lead to longevity, but cannot by itself really achieve the immortality that people so greatly desire. To achieve this you also need to develop who you are and in particular, like the Eight Immortals, be willing to take on the pompous, the oppressive and the corrupt. In Chinese thought immortality is not just a personal quest. It is about becoming and thus being part of the just order of the Tao, of the flow of nature and being opposed to all that hinders, obstructs or destroys the Way of the Tao.

4

REINCARNATION
AND KARMA

THE IDEA OF REBIRTH, transmigration of souls or full-blown reincarnation was unknown in China until the arrival of Buddhist missionaries in the late first century AD. Nor did the Chinese find this a very appealing belief at first. In fact, in order for it to be accepted by the Chinese at all, Buddhism had to make a choice between two key beliefs.

The main problem for the Chinese was how to square reincarnation with the other Buddhist teaching that there is no soul, no ultimate 'I'. For the central idea in classic Theravada Buddhism is that the existence of 'I' is the reason why suffering continues. In Theravada Buddhism, all suffering comes from the desire to find something which is 'me', which continues and has a life and meaning of its own. According to the original teachings of the Buddha, this is the ultimate illusion. Once we realise that there is no 'me', no 'I', no soul, then we can begin to appreciate that we are nothing more than the accumulated karma of actions which spring from trying to keep 'me' happy or give myself a sense of 'my' importance.

THE EIGHTFOLD NOBLE PATH

These ideas are best captured in the Buddha's Four Noble Truths, which, put simply, state:

1. Human life is full of suffering;

2. Suffering is caused by clinging to that which is passing, that which is ephemeral but which we try to make permanent – thus causing distress and suffering when it inevitably passes.

3. The path to the cessation of suffering is to let go of any desire to hold on to that which is impermanent. Thus will suffering from desire cease.

4. To do this, follow the Eightfold Noble Path and then suffering will cease.

The Eightfold Noble Path is essentially a pattern for living which ensures that, by gradual stages, one is freed from the illusions of desire and the struggle for permanence which give rise to suffering. The eight steps are:

1. *Right views* – to have a positive mind which reflects on what is good around you.

2. *Right thoughts* – to care for others and to be compassionate.

3. *Right speech* – not to lie nor to say anything which will cause harm.

4. *Right action* – not to kill, injure or steal.

5. *Right livelihood* – to engage in work which does no harm, such as being a butcher, or which cheats others.

6. *Right effort* – to follow the teachings of the Buddha and to walk the Eightfold Path.

7. *Right mindfulness* – to be aware of what you are thinking and doing.

8. *Right concentration* – this is the state of being aware of your non-existence, which comes as a result of truly following the Eightfold Path.

The concept that 'I' does not exist has perplexed those who encountered the Buddha's teaching from the time of the Buddha himself. These two accounts may offer some help.

'I am' is an imagining; 'I am this' is an imagining; 'I will be' ... 'I will not be' ... is an imagining. When the sage has gone beyond all imagining he is called at peace. The sage at peace is not born, does not age, is unagitated, is unobstructed. He has nothing of which to be born. Not being born, how could he age? Not ageing, how could he die? Not dying, how could he be agitated? Not being agitated, how could he be obstructed?

Majjhima Nikaya

In other words, if there is no action arising from desire there is no karma, which means there is no need to be reborn to wear off the karma gathered in the last life; so there is no birth and thus no death. This is not an easy concept, as this next quotation explores.

The wandering ascetic Vacchagotta visited the Exalted One ... and asked:
'How is it, master Gotama, does self exist?'
When this was said the Exalted One was silent.
'But then, master Gotama, does self not exist?'
For a second time the Exalted One was silent.
Then the wandering ascetic Vacchagotta got up from his seat and went away.
Now not long after he had gone, the Venerable Ananda asked the Exalted One:
'How is it, sir, that when the Exalted One was asked a question by the wandering ascetic Vacchagotta, he did not answer?'

*'If, Ananda, when asked by the wandering ascetic
Vacchagotta "Does self exist?" I had replied "Self exists",
would that have been in conformity with the understanding
that all things are non-self? If when asked by the wander-
ing ascetic Vacchagotta "Does self not exist?" I had replied,
"Self does not exist" then, Ananda, the bewildered
Vacchagotta would be even more bewildered, thinking,
"Formerly I surely had a self, but now I have not!"'*

Samyutta Nikaya

THE DESIRE FOR PERSONAL SALVATION

The response of the Chinese to this idea was not far from the
expected response of the wandering ascetic Vacchagotta – total
incomprehension and thus almost total lack of interest! Putting it
bluntly, Buddhism had to abandon any attempt to get the idea of
non-self across to the vast majority of Chinese because they could
not see that it had any relevance. In a culture where the body is
believed to have two different kinds of souls, seven in total, and
where the ancestor soul is worshipped, the notion that the soul
does not exist, that 'I' does not exist, was quite impossible. So the
Chinese ditched it in favour of other aspects of Buddhism which
they found more exciting or appealing. Of these, reincarnation
was one while the other was a natural corollary of this, the love for
and of the compassionate bodhisattvas and buddhas.

When Buddhism began to arrive in China, the pursuit of
personal salvation and redemption had just begun to surface.
Until around the first century AD, most Chinese had accepted that
they were of little significance and that concerns about the afterlife or about personal happiness and salvation were best left in
the hands of the emperors and the religious specialists. But after
this time the desire for personal salvation, for personal meaning,
had grown. Signs of this are the emergence of various divination
practices which indicate a belief that your life is worthwhile; your
life has meaning; and the gods or ancestors have something
special in store for you.

This search for personal meaning and salvation takes its first major form in the Five Bushels branch of Taoism which emerged in the second century AD under Chang Tao Ling, who is often called the founder figure of popular Taoism. The Five Bushels refers to the quantity of rice paid as a membership fee. And becoming a member was quite dramatic. You had to confess your sins and crimes, which were written down on paper and ceremonially burned. This freed you from the consequences of your past and the group then gave you a lifestyle built upon Taoist teachings which promised happiness in this life and beyond.

So, for the first time in recorded history in China, salvation was available through personal action and choice. And it was because of the newly discovered sense of self that the non-self teaching of Buddhism went down like a lead balloon. But the new religion's proposition that you were the sum total of your past actions, and the fact that it said you could break this cycle of birth, death, rebirth through good deeds and purifying yourself, was much more attractive.

It was a slow process. The Buddhists first had to convince people that their present state was the result of bad actions in past lives, and then had to offer a way of escaping from the consequences of these actions. Had it not been for the rise of the Taoist repentance culture, it seems unlikely that Buddhism would have managed to obtain much of a hold on the Chinese world. This is clear from the fact that the earliest Buddhist scriptures, translations from the Sanskrit originals, used Taoist terms extensively.

THE MAHAYANA TRADITION

As a result of all this, interest grew in a different form of Buddhism. Put simply, the original Theravada Buddhism that had been brought to China teaches the non-existence of self, and that the path to enlightenment and release is essentially an individual one which few achieve. Mahayana, in contrast, teaches that through the saving actions of enlightened beings who have deferred their own entry into Nirvana in order to stay and help suffering life on Earth, it is possible to receive help in escaping the consequences of your karma.

The title Mahayana means 'Great Vehicle'. Mahayanists often refer to the Theravada tradition as Hinayana or 'Lesser Vehicle.' This reflects Mahayana Buddhism's view of itself as able to carry many more people to salvation, to enlightenment or to escape from the terrors of rebirth than its Theravada counterpart.

The discovery of Mahayana opened the doors to popular Buddhism in China in a quite extraordinary way. The arrival of the salvationary Buddhism of the bodhisattvas dates from around the turn of the fifth and sixth centuries AD. Its effect is neatly captured in the rock carvings at Longmen, near Louyang. Those dated between 500 and 540 AD show the historical Buddha, the centre point of the Theravada tradition, as the most popular. There are 43 dedications to him, with 35 to the future Buddha Maitraya, 8 to the salvationary Buddha Amida and 22 to the bodhisattva of mercy, Kuan Yin. But from 650 to 690 AD, the dedications reflect a very different picture. Only 8 dedications are to the historical Buddha and 11 to the future Buddha Maitraya while 103 are to the salvationary Buddha Amida and 44 are to the bodhisattva of mercy, Kuan Yin.

So why the shift? Quite simply because, in the Mahayana tradition, reincarnation is transformed from something terrifying to something positive.

SAVED FROM SUFFERING

Reincarnation has been a source of terror for many generations of Chinese. It is not the nice, sanitised version which many in the West may imagine, of being an Egyptian princess in one life, then a member of the Roman aristocracy in another, a medieval knight in another, and so on. First and foremost, Chinese tradition teaches that no one can recall their past lives. Secondly, to be constantly dying, being born and dying again is the despair of many: it means being caught in a wheel of suffering and stress without visible end. There is nothing romantic or exciting about this belief for most people who have grown up in a culture of rebirth. Add to this the particularly gruesome accounts of what awaits the soul each time it dies, in the form of the Ten Hells with their dreadful punishments, and reincarnation becomes a curse which you will try to escape or break if you possibly can.

This is immensely important to understand. There is no romance in Chinese reincarnation, only pain and suffering. There is nothing exciting about constant rebirth, just a desperate desire to break this pattern of misery. This is one of the reasons why the Chinese have always kept open a number of options about the afterlife, ranging from becoming an ancestor spirit to the belief that the Judges of Hell can be bribed. Without such possibilities, the afterlife of punishment and rebirth is a terrifying prospect.

It is not just the fear of what lies in the afterworld. It is also the fear that, because you have acted badly in the past life, you will be given a new life which is worse than this one. Remember, for the vast majority of people in China down the ages, life has been almost unbearably tough. The thought that it could be even worse in the next life is frightening to put it mildly. Chinese Buddhism is vague about whether you come back as an animal if you have behaved very badly. Some traditions believe this, others don't. There tends to be a kind of evolutionary scale in reincarnation and it is unusual to regress to animal from human, or from animal to insect. Instead, what is believed to happen is that you will come back as someone with a physical handicap or in a very poor family. Physically handicapped people are still viewed askance by many Chinese even today, because it is believed that their handicap is a sign of an evil past life.

So the coming of the salvationary form of Buddhism, the emergence of faith in buddhas and bodhisattvas who can rescue you from this wheel of perpetual suffering, was a wonderful thing. This is why the *Lotus Sutra* is the most popular Buddhist text in China, for it offers a wonderful vision of how faith in the compassionate Buddha and in the bodhisattvas such as Kuan Yin can save you from the Hells and the terrors of rebirth.

At the heart of Chinese Buddhism lies two visions. The first is of the terror of reincarnation: of the dreadfulness of karma and the horrors of the consequences of your actions in this life and the judgement awaiting you in the next. But alongside this lies the vision of the Compassionate Ones, those who will reach down and pull true believers to safety, even carrying them off to the Land of Bliss and Happiness, the Western Paradise of Amida Buddha, where there is no more rebirth and so no more pain.

*Kuan Yin, the
bodhisattva of mercy.*

The core of this is the bodhisattva's vow to save all suffering life
(see below). This idea finds its greatest expression in the *Lotus
Sutra* and the bodhisattva of mercy, Kuan Yin.

THE BODHISATTVA OF MERCY

Having now seen what terrrifying images the believer was
presented with, it may be a little easier to understand why the
bodhisattvas are so adored and so ardently worshipped. One of
the most popular is Kuan Yin, who, it is believed, made a
commitment to save suffering life. In Chapter 25 of the *Lotus
Sutra*, the bodhisattva promises: 'If any, carried away by a flood,
call upon the bodhisattva's name, they will immediately reach the
shallows ... or if anyone cries who is in deadly peril by the

sword, the sword will be snapped asunder. If wicked demons attack, the one who cries will become invisible to them.'

This is what the bodhisattva can do for you in this life. But what about the next life? The text continues with this promise:

> *Every evil state of existence,*
> *hells and ghosts and animals,*
> *sorrows of birth, age, disease, death,*
> *all this will be ended for him [who calls upon the bodhissattva].*
> *True Regard, serene Regard,*
> *Far-reaching, wise Regard,*
> *Regard of pity, Regard compassionate,*
> *Ever longed for, ever looked for*
> *In radiance ever pure and serene!*

The text promises that if someone constantly thinks upon the bodhisattva, then, even if he is cast into the fiery pits of Hell, they will become a cool pool of tranquillity. Here is the vision which offers hope of escape from the horrors of Hell, or, to be more precise perhaps, from the horrors of what we make of our lives. In the compassionate bodhisattva, be that the goddess Kuan Yin, the Buddha Amida or any of the other Compassionate Ones, lies the hope of salvation and of liberation. It is a beautiful image: the selfless outpouring of love and merit to redeem the souls of those who would otherwise be locked forever into the wheel of rebirth and of suffering.

Kuan Yin is often depicted with a thousand eyes and hands, constantly looking for those she can help, constantly offering her hand to those in peril. The bodhisattvas are believed to visit the Hells, seeking those whom they can rescue, those who have faith in them and have sought their protection while alive. This is why in Chinese Buddhist temples the historical Buddha, the prince Siddhartha Gautama, is of little significance. He usually occupies a shrine near the main entrance, in one of the lesser halls. As you penetrate further and further into the heart of the temple, you come to the bodhisattvas and the Buddha of the Western Paradise, Amida, who can pluck souls straight into his paradise if they sincerely believe. For they are the living heart of the faith; they alone can bring you to peace at death and not to torment or to rebirth.

5

OF HELLS AND REBIRTH

EARTH-PRISONS

THE IDEA OF HELL – or to be more accurate, of a number of Hells, each with its own terrible punishments – was unknown in China until the arrival of Buddhism. Indeed, there was no need for such a concept. If there was no reincarnation, there was no need for the soul to be judged, purified and then reborn.

In earliest Chinese thought, it would appear that the souls went to places of comfort. The po remained with the body and passed away after three years, while the hun ascended to Heaven to be seated in order of precedence by the Supreme Ruler of Heaven or the Yellow Emperor, a deified early ruler. In other accounts, such as the fourth-century BC philosopher Chuang Tzu, the afterlife is described in very vague terms as the Yellow Springs – a subterranean region where the dead wander in a hazy sort of way – though he also talks, albeit flippantly, about a kind of reincarnation. The notion of the Yellow Springs is not dissimilar to the Shades in Greek mythology or Sheol in ancient Hebraic thought.

When Buddhism arrived in force in China, during the third to fourth centuries AD, it brought with it a whole panoply of beliefs about the afterlife, prominent amongst which was the notion of Hells. The word the Chinese used for this idea, Ti Yu, means Earth-prison, and it underlines their purpose. These are not places in which the departed languish for ever. They are places of punishment, with prescribed periods during which the soul is tortured and punished in order that it can then move on into the next life, purged or punished for the deeds of this life. That is why the term 'prison' is used. That said, there are some crimes for which the punishment is endless – the exact crimes differ from account to account.

This 'Earth-prison' was also the region where judgement could take place. Based on what you had done in this life, you were judged and an appropriate rebirth decreed for you. The Hells were – are – a necessary part of the process of reincarnation.

The first evidence of the notion of Hell coming into China is found in sutras translated by the Buddhist priest An Shih Kao, who brought them from Parthia (today's Middle East) in AD 148. Originally the texts refer to eight Hells, all of which were hot. But as Buddhism expanded in China, the notion of a parallel eight cold Hells emerged. These were then topped and tailed by a Hell of Arrival and a Hell of Departure – really Judgement Halls. This gives a grand total of eighteen Buddhist Hells, though in pictures normally only ten are shown.

By the sixth to seventh century AD Taoism had taken up the themes of the Hells in its own literature and practices, but not as wholeheartedly as Buddhism. While Buddhism has produced much material – and still does today – which illustrates the penalties in Hell for certain crimes or actions, Taoism still holds the view that retribution takes place primarily in this life, or is passed on to your descendants. It does not look to the life after death as being the principal place where you suffer or make up for your actions in this world.

The two faiths' texts illustrate this difference. For example, the Buddhist text *Leng Yen Ching* offers the following cheerful news: 'Sexual desire creates hot iron beds ... Carnality creates a fiery pit, craving creates bitter cold, anger inflames and becomes hills of knives.' All these are to be found in the Hells of Buddhism. But Taoism, through its most influential text, the *Tai Shang Kan Ying Pien*, written in the eleventh century AD, still posits a world view in which punishment comes in this life: 'Lao Tzu says: "Fortune and misfortune are the results of our actions. Reward and retribution follow us like shadows."'

The text then lists a vast array of evil deeds, such as: 'Taking advantage of kind people ... punishing people unjustly ... shooting animals that fly and run. Frightening worms and animals that crawl ... breaking up families ... vandalism and setting fire to buildings.' The punishment for these offences is as follows:

> *If you do these kinds of evil things then years will be taken from your life, depending on the seriousness of your evil deeds. When all the years have been taken from you, you die. If you have debts [that is, debts of bad karma by such actions], your children and grandchildren will have to pay them. If you have taken money and possessions from others, your spouse and children will suffer the consequences as well ... If you kill innocent people, you will suffer the retribution of violent death.*

The origins of the Buddhist Hells lie in India, amongst the beliefs of the Vedic culture from which Buddhism emerged. However, it is in China that they come into full flower, with graphic descriptions and vivid illustrations to ram home the message of the cost of sinfulness. Today you are likely to find them portrayed in sculpture, statues or painting in Taoist temples. Indeed, complete sets of prints of the Ten Hells can be purchased through the China Taoist Association bookshops, while Buddhist temples sell books outlining the punishments inflicted upon you according to a table of sins, similar to those on p. 16.

THE EIGHTEEN HELLS

So what are all these Hells and how does one get out of them? The full set of eighteen is sharply defined in the famous novel *Monkey*, or *Journey to the West*, written by the Buddhist writer Wu Cheng En in the mid-sixteenth century. One of the most popular books in China, it describes the journey of an historical figure, the monk Hsuan Tsang, who in AD 629 set out on a secret mission to India to collect Buddhist sutras and relics, a journey which took sixteen years. Around this real journey grew a vast array of myths featuring legendary companions who were able to achieve redemption for past crimes by accompanying the monk. His assistants are Monkey, Pigsy and Sandy, animal beings who through adventures and pluck, not to mention pure cheek, fight against the devils and demons and wicked Taoist monks who try to stop the monk's journey.

Early in the novel there is a graphic description of a visit to the eighteen Hells of Buddhism by the Emperor Tai Tsung, who had been summoned there to answer charges of abuse of power. He manages to escape by having an extra twenty years added to the length of his life in the Register of Life.

When Tai Tsung first enters Hell he is met by someone who was an actual judge in his own earthly empire, but upon dying became a judge in the underworld. This was often thought to happen, and there are even stories of people petitioning to be made judges when they die. Tai Tsung asks the judge to explain the eighteen Hells, which he does in these words:

> 'The Hanging-by-the-Sinews Hell, the Hell of Injustice and
>   the Hell of the Pit of Fire.
> Loneliness and desolation,
> Misery and suffering.
> All those here committed the thousand lower sins,
> And were sent here for punishment after death.
>
> The Fengdu Hell, the Tongue-Extraction Hell, the Flaying
>   Hell:
> Howling and wailing,
> Terrible anguish.

They offended against Heaven by not being loyal or filial;
They have Buddha-mouths but snake hearts, so fell down here.

The Grinding Hell, the Pounding Hell, the Hell of Drawing
    and Quartering.
Skin and flesh ripped and torn,
lips rubbed away till the teeth show.
In the blindness of their hearts they did evil things;
For all their fine words they harmed others in secret.

The Ice Hell, the Skin-shedding Hell, the Disembowelling
    Hell.
Filthy faces and matted hair,
Frowning foreheads and sad eyes.
They all used false measures to cheat the foolish,
Thus piling up disasters for themselves.

The Oil-Cauldron Hell, the Hell of Blackness, the Hell of
    the Mountain of Knives.
Shivering and trembling,
In terrible agony;
Because they used violence against the good
They cower and hunch their shoulders in their suffering.

The Hell of the Pool of Blood, the Avichi Hell, the Hell of
    the Steelyard Beam,
Where skin is pulled away from the bone,
Arms are broken and tendons cut.
Because they killed for gain,
Butchering living creatures,
They fell into these torments that will not end in a
    thousand years;
They will always lie here, never to escape.

Everyone of them is tightly bound,
Knotted and roped.
Red-faced demons,
And black-faced demons,
Are sent with their long halberds and short swords.
Ox-headed fiends,
And horse-faced fiends,
With iron clubs and brazen hammers,
Beat them till their wincing faces flow with blood,

As they call on Heaven and Earth and get no answer.
Let no man alive have any illusions:
The devils carry out their orders and release nobody.
Good and evil will always be rewarded:
It is only a question of time.'

Buddhists introduced the notion of hells and depicted them visually and the Taoists took them up and described them in detail in their writings. The Taoist Hells have been the subject of many descriptions, usually in the form of a journey undertaken by a wrongly seized soul which is then released once the mistake has been realised. The classic description of them is found in a Taoist text dating from around 1070; the *Yu Li Chao Chuan*, written by Tan Chih. It describes a visit made by that monk to the Ten Hells, and what follows is a condensed version of his account.

THE FIRST COURT OF HELL

King Chin Kuang is in charge of the First Court of Hell, where he supervises the Register of Life and Death and sits in judgement on all souls that descend to Hell. His court is to be found in the Great Ocean, beyond the Wu Chiao Rocks, far to the west of the murky road that leads to the Yellow Springs. If someone comes before him having led a life of such virtue that their good deeds outweigh their bad or balance against them, they will be immediately returned to life. If they have earned such promotion they will be reborn in an even better form than in their past life.

But those who have committed more bad deeds than good are sent to a place called the Terrace of the Mirror of Sins. Here they are confronted by every animal or bird or fish which they caused to be killed to provide them with food; every person they ever harmed; every wickedness they have committed. Then they realise the truth of the proverb:

Ten Thousand taels of gold cannot be taken from this life;
But every crime will tell its tale upon the judgement day.

Once its crimes have been revealed in the Mirror of Sin, the soul

King Chin Kuang records the fate of the souls in The Register of Life and Death.

is judged and sent to the appropriate Hell or Hells to begin its journey of suffering, which for some will never end. If any priest, Buddhist or Taoist, enters this court having been paid to say prayers but not having bothered to do them properly, he will be sent to a special part of Hell called the Completion of Prayer and there finish all prayers left unfinished. Only then can he be judged.

To avoid this punishment, turn to the north and vow to abstain from evil and to think only of the good that you can do. Study the teachings of the Buddha, for they were given to save you from such terrors.

THE SECOND COURT OF HELL

King Chu Chiang rules the Second Court. His Hell is vast, and contains sixteen sections.

In the first is nothing but black clouds and unending sandstorms. In the second, mud and filth. In the third, terrible cold. In the fourth, gnawing hunger. In the fifth, burning thirst. In the sixth, blood and putridity. In the seventh, boiling water. In the eighth, repeated dunking in boiling water. In the ninth, the souls are placed in iron cases. In the tenth, they are stretched upon a rack until they reach regulation length! In the eleventh they are constantly pecked by fowl. In the twelfth, they are given only rivers of lime to drink. In the thirteenth they are hacked to pieces. In the fourteenth, they must climb trees whose leaves are as sharp as swords. In the fifteenth they are attacked by foxes and wolves, and in the sixteenth they live in ice and snow.

Knawing hunger and burning thirst are amongst the terrors of the Second Court of Hell.

Here come those who have done things such as leading astray young people and then escaping punishment by taking to a monastery as a monk; those who practise as doctors without any training; those who injure a fellow creature in any way; those who, knowing that one of the partners in a forthcoming marriage is a bad person, fails to say so.

To escape the consequences of such actions you must in your lifetime tend the sick, feed the hungry, give alms to those in need and ensure that no harm comes to even the smallest of creatures through your actions or desires.

THE THIRD COURT OF HELL

This court is ruled by King Sung Ti and lies at the bottom of the Great Ocean, in the Hell of Black Bonds. It too has sixteen sections. The first contains nothing but salt, which the dead eat and are driven mad by it. The second is a place where the dead wear yokes and are bound. In the third they are forever speared through the ribs. In the fourth their faces are scraped away with knives. The fifth involves having all the fat removed from their bodies. In the sixth their hearts and livers are squeezed, while in the seventh their eyes are gouged out. In the eighth they are flayed alive and in the ninth their feet are cut off. In the tenth toenails and fingernails are extracted, while in the eleventh their blood is sucked out. In the twelfth they hang upside down and in the thirteenth they are bitten by insects and reptiles. In the fifteenth their thighs are beaten and finally in the sixteenth their hearts are attacked.

Those who are thrown in here are such as would interfere with someone's feng shui in order to bring bad luck; those who accept payment but do not do the work; those who forget or lose the record of where their family is buried; and those who drive others to commit crimes – these souls come here even if they have built up merit as well.

To avoid these punishments, cease to take lives; become a vegetarian and teach your children to do so also. Harm no creature, insect or beast and you will avoid this Hell.

King Sung Ti surveys the souls being punished in the Third Court of Hell.

THE FOURTH COURT OF HELL

The ruler of the Fourth Court is Wu Kuan, Lord of the Five Senses. In the first sector the dead are tortured with water continuously, and in the second they must kneel on iron chains and broken bamboo. In the third their hands are constantly plunged into boiling water, while in the fourth they are sweated until they swell. The fifth sector involves having their bones pulled out, and in the sixth they are prodded with a trident and their skin rubbed raw. In the seventh holes are drilled into them, and in the eighth they must sit on spikes. In the ninth they wear iron coats, while in the tenth they are crushed under great weights. The eleventh involves having their eyes put out and the twelfth means having

Tax evaders and the sellers of counterfeit goods are amongst those condemned to the Fourth Court of Hell.

dust stuffed in their mouths. In the thirteenth they must take dreadful medicine and in the fourteenth they try to stand but cannot. In the fifteenth their mouths are constantly pricked, and finally in the sixteenth their body is buried under stones, leaving just the head visible.

Those who are brought here have cheated customs or the tax collector; have sold counterfeit goods; have failed to be thoughtful to cripples; have had medicine but would not spare it for the sick; the poor who have not behaved as they should; and the rich who have had no thought for the poor.

To avoid these punishments, set your mind against sin. Vow only to do what is virtuous and publish books which set a good example. Such charitable actions will help save you.

THE FIFTH COURT OF HELL

Here sits the benevolent king, Yen Lo. His true place is in the First Court, but from compassion he moved to the Fifth Court – for here come those who are the most hardened and evil of souls. They have already been through seven days of terrible torture in the preceding four Hells. It is here in the Fifth Court that their deepest crime is revealed by themselves, and this brings its own punishment in one of the sixteen sectors. Here they are allowed one last look back at the world they have left. They see the fruits of their evil: descendants who care nothing for them; children gone astray; property sold and broken up; friends forgetting them.

The Fifth Court of Hell is the destination of the most hardened and evil souls.

They are crushed, poisoned, beaten and flayed before being sent to one of the sixteen sectors. To the first go those who failed to worship and atheists, while in the second are found those who hurt or killed living beings. The third contains those who reneged on vows, and the fourth those who followed fraudulent preachers and magicians. In the fifth are those who bullied the weak but who kow-towed to the strong, and in the sixth are those who put the blame for their mistakes on others. In the seventh are those who were immoral, while in the eighth are those who harmed others in order to benefit themselves. Those who were so mean as never to help others are in the ninth, and in the tenth are those who inveigle the weak into stealing. In the eleventh are those who plotted revenge, while in the twelfth are those who sell drugs which harm people. In the thirteenth are found deceivers, and in the fourteenth those who love fighting. In the fifteenth are those who envy the wise and good, and in the sixteenth are those sunk in vice, slanderers and others of their ilk.

Many other crimes are punished here, such as not believing in karma or slandering the Buddha; failing to teach what was right or damaging religious books – too many to list. But all end up here for punishment.

THE SIXTH COURT OF HELL

The ruler here is King Pien Cheng, and his court is found at the bottom of the Great Ocean to the north of the Wu Chiao Rocks.

In the first sector the souls are made to kneel on lumps of lead, and in the second they sink up to their necks in filth. They are pounded to pieces in the third, while in the fourth they are forced to chew on nails. In the fifth they are gnawed by rats, while in the sixth, surrounded by thorns, they are bitten by locusts. The seventh involves being crushed to a mush, and the eighth means having their skin cut and then beaten raw. In the ninth their mouths are filled with fire, while in the tenth they are burned by fire. The eleventh consists of dreadful smells, and the twelfth involves being butted and trodden on by oxen and horses. In the thirteenth their hearts are cut, and in the fourteenth they have their heads rubbed off. In the fifteenth they are cut in two, while

Being knawed by rats and bitten by locusts are amongst the punishments of the Sixth Court of Hell.

in the sixteenth their skin is removed and they are rolled up on to spills.

To this Hell come those who attack Heaven or the Earth; those who make a mess near temples; those who blaspheme; those who attack religious images; and those who commit other heinous crimes against religion.

To avoid these punishments, take a vow of abstinence from all that depraves and corrupts. Seek to convert others to the Path of the Buddha and you will escape these horrors.

THE SEVENTH COURT OF HELL

This court, deep in the Great Ocean, north-west of the Wu Chiao Rocks, is ruled by King Tai Shan.

In the first section the souls are made to drink their own blood, while in the second, their legs are pierced and burned. In the third they have their chests cut open, and in the fourth their hair is torn out. In the fifth they are eaten by dogs, while in the sixth they have great stones placed upon their heads. In the seventh their skulls are pierced, and in the eighth their clothes are always on fire. Pigs attack them in the ninth, and in the tenth they are pecked by birds of great size. In the eleventh they are hung up and beaten on their feet, while in the twelfth they have their tongues pulled out and their jaws drilled. In the thirteenth they are disembowelled, while in the fourteenth they are trampled by mules and bitten by badgers. In the fifteenth their fingers are crushed by hot irons, and finally in the sixteenth they are boiled in oil.

Grave robbers and slave dealers are amongst the condemned of the Seventh Court of Hell.

To this dreadful place come those who have kidnapped people for sale as slaves; who robbed graves; who cheated with others in gambling; who beat their slaves unjustly; and who disobeyed their elders.

To avoid these punishments, every day pray earnestly and repent of all that you have done wrong. Publish edifying texts for the people, and you will escape these terrors.

THE EIGHTH COURT OF HELL

The ruler of the Eighth Court is King Tu Shih, who dwells at the bottom of the Great Ocean, east of the Wu Chiao Rocks.

King Tu Shih presides over the tortures of the Eighth Court of Hell.

In the first sector the souls are rolled down mountains in carts, and in the second they are placed in huge saucepans. In the third they are chopped up, while in the fourth they have their orifices blocked up. In the fifth their uvulas are cut off, and in the sixth they are dumped in filth. Their extremities are cut off in the seventh, and their heart, kidneys and livers fried in the eighth. In the ninth their marrow is cauterised, while in the tenth their bowels are cut out. In the eleventh they are consumed by fire inside, and in the twelfth they are disembowelled. Their chests are torn open in the thirteenth, and in the fourteenth their skulls are cracked and their teeth pulled. In the fifteenth they are hacked to pieces, and in the sixteenth they are pierced with prongs.

71

Here those who have been unfilial are brought; also those who cause their parents distress and those who practise black magic.

To avoid these punishments, publish edifying texts of religious teachings and you will be pardoned.

THE NINTH COURT OF HELL

The ruler here is King Peng Teng, and his Hell is situated at the bottom of the Great Ocean, south-west of the Wu Chiao Rocks.

Murderers and arsonists are amongst those suffering in the Ninth Court of Hell.

In the first sector the souls are beaten and their bodies burned, while in the second their bones are hit. The third consists of ducks eating the livers of the damned, while in the fourth dogs devour them. In the fifth they are splashed with boiling oil, and in the sixth their heads are crushed. In the seventh their brains are taken out and their heads filled with hedgehogs. The eighth consists of having their heads steamed and their brains scraped, while the ninth involves being dragged around by sheep until they fall apart. In the tenth they are crushed, and in the eleventh their hearts are ground to dust. In the twelfth they are tortured by water, and in the thirteenth they are stung by wasps. The fourteenth involves torture by ants and maggots, the fifteenth by being cooked, and the sixteenth by poison from snakes.

Here are brought those who in their lives committed terrible crimes such as murder, who were arsonists or who published evil books.

To avoid these punishments, fast regularly. Buy up all bad and corrupting books and burn them. Instead, publish edifying texts. If you can afford it, buy up the printing presses where evil and pornographic books are printed and destroy them or convert them to good deeds. These actions will save you.

THE TENTH COURT OF HELL

Here is the Hell of King Chuan Lun, in the place known as the Dark Land, east of the Wu Chiao Rocks and just opposite the gate back to this world. Here are six bridges, one of gold, one of silver, one of jade, one of stone, one of smooth wood and one of rough planks. All souls must pass over one of these bridges; the choice of bridge depends upon where they are on the scale of reincarnation.

When the souls have passed through the appropriate Hells and sections of each Hell and have been purified of their evil, they all come to this last Hell to be judged. In the light of what they did, they will be reborn according to their just deserts. But before they cross one of the bridges and return to life they must first visit the Terrace of Oblivion where Meng Po, a wise old woman who once lived on Earth, now lives. She prepares for them a drink which removes all memory of the past.

This became necessary because there were unscrupulous men who tried to trick innocent women. These men claimed that they remembered being married to certain women in former lives, and claimed that this meant they could sleep with them now. So Meng Po mixes her drink and makes all souls forget eveything that has happened in past lives. Those who claim to be able to remember are thus proven liars.

The souls, once their new life has been decided, are brought across the bridges and then thrust into the stream of red which flows under the Bitter Bamboo Bridge. This stream carries them into their next birth, and great is the sorrow of all those who must once again return to life.

Once the souls have been purified, they are judged in the Tenth Court of Hell before being reborn.

WAYS OUT OF HELL

It will be quite clear by now that the Chinese Buddhist and, by adoption, Taoist visions of the afterlife are pretty terrible. The extraordinary catalogue of fantasies about cruelty and torture are enough to make even the strong-stomached stop and think. This, of course, was one of their purposes. Unfortunately, as in so many religions, much of what has just been described consists of the sick thoughts of unpleasant monks and nuns who wanted to inflict suffering on those who did what they disliked. Nevertheless these images have had a terrifyingly powerful effect on the imagination of the Chinese for well over a thousand years and you will find scenes from the Hells depicted in a variety of places, even in pleasure parks such as the Tiger Balm Gardens in Hong Kong and Singapore.

So what hope is there for the average person today? Well, apart from becoming an Immortal, which was explored in Chapter 4, there are two ways out – or, at least, one way out and one way of alleviating the worst of what the Hells have to offer. Let's start with alleviating the consequences of what has been done in this life.

The whole of the Chinese Taoist and much of the popular Buddhist pantheon is modelled on Imperial institutions. The administration system of city officials, town administrators and local ward officers was replicated in the city gods, town gods and ward gods. Thus popular belief saw the rulers and officials of the afterlife as simply more powerful versions of the same people who made their everyday life in this world hard to bear. And they assumed that they could be dealt with in much the same way as officials in this life – namely, bribery. If you could carry as much money and gold into the next life as possible, you could bribe the officials to treat you more leniently. It didn't mean you could escape punishment altogether, but you could avoid some of the nastier ones or have to endure them for a shorter period.

This is why, at Chinese funerals and festivals associated with the dead, you will find people burning money. They burn paper money in denominations of anything from $50 million to $100 million, in bundles of hundreds and hundreds of such denominations – all the notes being made out to the ruler of the Fifth Court, Yen Lo. These bear his image and after being burned are 'banked' in the Bank of Hell – hence their name, Bank of Hell notes. Alongside these will be paper models of gold bars and silver ingots. These too are often burned, accompanied by prayers beseeching the gods to look favourably upon the departed. When the soul arrives in Hell with a considerable bank balance he or she is able to bribe the officials and pass more swiftly through the rigours of the Earth-prisons.

There are also certain home comforts provided by the family. Paper models of servants, of houses, cars, TV sets, videos, computers and other essentials are burned at the funeral to provide all that may be needed in the afterlife. Much of this will be utilised by the po soul, whereas it is the hun soul which goes through the Hells. Either way, these items are sent to make sure that the ancestor is comfortable and will not take out his anger at being dead upon the living.

So one way through Hell is by well-placed bribes to the officials whom one meets *en route* to rebirth. But none of this can actually help you avoid the fate you have created for yourself. This is why the bodhisattvas of mercy and compassion are so important. Without the hope that Kuan Yin might rescue you and transport you to Amida Buddha's Western Paradise, many people would face death with little short of total terror. It is the contrast between the Hells and compassion which fuels popular Buddhism and popular religion in general.

6

SALVATION

BEING ONE WITH THE TAO

IN CHAPTER 5 we wandered into the often horrific world of the Ten and Eighteen Hells. It is not a place for the squeamish, and not a world that the average Chinese person ever wanted to visit for too long.

To avoid this terrifying world or its worst effects was one of the driving forces behind the emergence of the compassionate bodhisattvas. But there is an even more fundamental way of escaping the rigours of Hell, and that is to find one's true place within the ebb and flow of life as expressed through the visions of the cosmos found in Taoism, and to a certain degree in Buddhism.

Much of what the Hells are imagined to have to correct is an inflated or wrong understanding of our own significance. We have seen how, in ancestor worship, one's place within a wider system of values and priorities – the family – is paramount. Underpinning this and to some extent relegating this is the world view, or rather the cosmic view, of Chinese philosophy and religions which places the whole of our meaning within the meaning of existence itself.

This is important. The strength of Chinese belief is that it combines the supernatural with the natural but ultimately puts the natural above the supernatural. For example, all the kings and judges of Hell will themselves be reborn or transformed and eventually the Hells will all pass away, returning to be one with the principle of the universe, the Tao. Nothing is forever except the Tao, the Way of Nature.

The essence of the Chinese world view, both Taoist and in many ways also Confucian and Chinese Buddhist, is found in the opening chapter of the *Tao Te Ching*, compiled around the fourth century BC. The Tao as origin and meaning is expressed most beautifully here:

> *The Tao that can be talked about is not the true Tao.*
> *The name that can be named*
> *is not the eternal Name.*
> *Everything in the universe comes out of Nothing.*
>
> *Nothing – the nameless*
> *is the beginning;*
> *While Heaven, the mother*
> *is the creatrix of all things.*
>
> *Follow the nothingness of the Tao,*
> *and you can be like it, not needing anything,*
> *seeing the wonder and the root of everything.*
>
> *And even if you cannot grasp this nothingness,*
> *you can still see something of the Tao in everything.*
>
> *These two are the same*
> *only called by different names*
>
> *– and both are mysterious and wonderful.*
>
> *All mysteries are Tao, and Heaven is their mother:*
> *She is the gateway and the womb-door.*

The role of humanity in this cosmic view of the Tao is both elevated and yet also servant-like. In chapter 42 of the *Tao Te Ching* is the following vision of the place and significance of human beings:

> *The Tao*
> *gives birth to the One:*
> *The One*
> *gives birth to the two;*
> *The Two*
> *gives birth to the three –*
> *The Three give birth to every living thing.*
> *All things are held in yin and carry yang:*
> *And they are held together in the ch'i of teeming energy.*

The One is the emanation of the ultimate Origin, the Tao. The two are yin and yang, the primal forces of life, one cold, wet and female and the other hot, fiery and male. The three are Heaven (yang), Earth (yin) and humanity.

TAOISM-BALANCING THE FORCES

In Chinese Taoist life and ritual this significant role as one of the three essential forces in the cosmos is expressed through the role that humans have in keeping the balance between the conflicting forces of yin and yang. If human beings act as they should, they help to regulate the world and indeed the cosmos. This was the role played by the Emperor as the Son of Heaven when each year he went to make sacrifices and obeisance to Heaven at the Temple of Heaven and then to the Earth at the Temple of the Earth. Here he stood and offered repentance for those actions of humanity which had disturbed the balance of yin and yang and the cosmos, often manifesting itself in earthquakes, floods or other disasters. Here also he sought the blessing of Heaven and Earth on the coming year and upon humanity.

In the liturgies of Taoism this is enacted at a more local level to this very day. It is a most important aspect of Taoism, and one which offers a fascinating model for Westerners to study and reflect upon. It suggests that the role of humans is of vital importance – not for our own sake, but for the sake of all existence. It is this servant model of our significance which underpins the Taoist approach to issues such as power or the environment. We are here to be a part of something greater, and to be a moral part. We are not here for self-aggrandisement.

The *Lich Tzu*, a text dating from around the third century BC puts this relationship very succinctly, using the term 'sage' to stand for humanity.

> *Heaven and Earth cannot achieve everything;*
> *The sage is not capable of everything;*
> *None of the myriad things [meaning all life] can be used*
> *   for everything.*

> *For this reason*
> *It is the office of Heaven to beget and to shelter,*
> *The office of Earth to shape and to support,*
> *The office of the sage to teach and reform.*
> *The office of each thing to perform its function.*

Through the Tao, all life is interconnected. What happens to me happens to the whole cosmos, and vice versa. Thus what I do, even symbolically, has impact upon the whole universe. This is why a liturgy celebrated in some remote parts of China is viewed as having cosmic significance. In about the fourth century BC the writer Chuang Tzu put it succinctly: 'Heaven and Earth were born at the same time I was, and the ten thousand things [all living beings] are one with me.'

The great fourth-century AD Taoist philosopher Ko Hung expresses what lies at the heart of the Taoist understanding of meditation and liturgy, prayer and ritual in fulfilling our role in the cosmos:

> *Here is what I have learned:*
> *He who knows the One has accomplished everything.*
> *He who knows the One knows all.*
> *For him who does not know the One, there is nothing he*
> *   can know.*

The Tao reveals itself first of all in the One.
It is therefore of incomparable value.

The One resides each in its own place, in Heaven, Earth
*   and Humanity.*
This is why we speak of the Three Ones ...

If we know how to preserve it, the One is there;
If we neglect it, the One is lost.
If we turn towards it, we find good fortune;
If we turn away from it, we meet disaster.
Those who know how to keep it will experience endless joy.
In those who lost it, life will dry up, their energies exhausted.

Chuang Tzu also puts in perspective the passing away of individual life by seeing it as part of the continuous flow of the Tao
which carries all before it. Thus both life and death are but part
of this flow, and not to be particularly marvelled at.

Chuang Tzu's wife died and Hui Tzu came to console him,
but Chuang Tzu was sitting, legs akimbo, bashing a
battered tub and singing.
*   Hui Tzu said, 'You lived as man and wife, she reared your*
children. At her death surely the least you should be doing
is to be on the verge of weeping, rather than banging the
tub and singing: this is not right!'
*   Chuang Tzu said, 'Certainly not. When she first died, I*
certainly mourned just like everyone else! However, I then
thought back to her birth and to the very roots of her being,
before she was born. Indeed, not just before she was born
but before the time when her body was created. Not just
before her body was created but before the very origin of
her life's breath. Out of all this, through the wonderful
mystery of change she was given her life's breath. Her life's
breath wrought a transformation and she had a body. Her
body wrought a transformation and she was born. Now
there is yet another transformation and she is dead. She is
like the four seasons in the way that spring, summer,
autumn and winter follow each other. She is now at peace,
lying in her chamber, but if I were to sob and cry it would
certainly appear that I could not comprehend the ways of
destiny. This is why I stopped.'

At a traditional Taoist funeral, elements of the cosmic theology and of the dismissive view of the difference between life and death are expressed, but so too is the notion of freeing the spirit of the departed from the consequences of their wrong actions here on earth. There is even one ceremony called the Attack on Hell. This is essentially an exorcism ritual, which uses military langauge to describe its actions. The Attack is a very dramatic ritual, involving mediums who often end by literally attacking a model of Hell, built like a fortress. They also engage in what sounds like heated debate with the forces of evil; the ghosts often act out in highly dramatic fashion their fights with such forces.

A model fortress is set up on a table, usually in the house of the dead person. Around this table assemble the members of the family and the priests and mediums. The fortress is a paper model of Hell, some of which are very elaborate indeed. In front of the fortress is placed a bowl of water so that the soul can wash itself once it escapes from the filth and horrors of Hell. After ritual prayers and the drama of debate comes the moment of the assault on the fortress, which can end with everyone in tears, ripping the paper to pieces. It can be a very therapeutic ritual.

These rituals have been affected by Buddhist beliefs about the various hells and the suffering which one endures. Before Taoism was influenced by Buddhism, Taoists thought that the period after death and before rebirth was fairly painless.

Yet there is still a sense in Taoism that the consequences of this life can be balanced by reflecting upon the truth of the Tao. By meditating and coming to a deeper understanding of the purpose and meaning of life – or conversely, according to Taoist ritual prayer, the meaninglessness of life and death: 'To transcend the difficulties of the Three Realms and obtain release from the five sufferings of the Earth-prisons, all turn to the scriptures of the Most High and, meditating purely, make obeisance.'

In a touching use of an actual Buddhist figure, albeit one which has accrued many Taoist deities' attributes to her, Taoism often calls upon the goddess of Mercy Kuan Yin to come to the aid of those suffering in Hell, or on their death beds. She is believed to be able to assist the soul or the dying person to pass straight into rebirth or even, if they have merited it, into the Paradise of Heaven. In Taoism, her salvationary role is very clear, though she shares it with many deities within Taoism. Yet her special role as one who will descend into Hell itself to rescue the departed is remembered in Taoist ritual and prayers.

This brings us to Buddhist prayers and notions of salvation, of life and death.

BUDDHISM – RESCUED BY COMPASSION

The concept of compassion in Buddhism is beautifully expressed in the poem by the Pure Land monk Yin Kuang (1861–1940). (The Pure Land is the land ruled over by Amida Buddha. Those who followed this tradition believed that they would go to the Pure Land at death as long as they truly believed and sincerely prayed.)

> *The mind and nature of common man*
> *Do not fall short of the Buddha's own;*
> *Illusion leads us all astray,*
> *We spin through endless life and death.*
>
> *Tathagata, moved by pity,*
> *Preached the dharma to receptive hearts:*
> *To each and every living thing,*
> *He pointed out the homeward road.*
>
> *Enlightenment has many doors,*
> *But two of them stand at the fore:*
> *Ch'an and Pure Land are their names –*
> *The simplest roads to reach release.*
>
> *With Ch'an there's no one but yourself,*
> *While Pure Land borrows Buddha's strength:*
> *When these are on a balance weighed,*
> *Pure Land seems suited to our needs.*
>
> *As crossing over boundless seas,*
> *No man without a trusty craft*
> *Can swiftly reach the other shore,*
> *His mind and poise still undisturbed ...*

Develop the enlightened mind
Let faith take root within your heart ...

Recite until, all motive gone,
To dwell [Amitabha] on Him is not to dwell ...!

Then when the end of life looms near
With help from Buddha's guiding hand,
Ascend straight to the highest plane
And learn the patience of birthlessness.

I give you now the key to every door:
Use every ounce of strength to live
With sincerity and reverence –
The fruits are marvellous indeed.

The hope of ascending direct to the Pure Land or the Paradise of the West (west is the mystical direction in Chinese belief, as the east is in Western thought) of Amida sustains many world-weary believers in this life. And who can blame them? This is a description of the Pure Land taken from the fourth-century AD Buddhist monk and writer Hui Yuan:

What words can do justice to the beauty and magnitude of
*   that pure and shining land?*
The place where the blossoms never fade with the passing
*   of the days,*
where the golden gates gleam as if purest water.
The land rises, terrace upon terrace
made of diamond steps and shining jade balustrades.
Here there is nothing but fragrant bowers
where the Utpala lotus opens freely.
Listen to the sweet music from the hills and the valleys
The praise of the Great Buddha from the mouths of the
*   birds.*

Here the years roll by in an endless chain,
Neither summer nor winter make their impact here.
Neither the heat of the sun nor the chill of ice
disturb the flow in this Pure Land.
The sky is filled with light and the trees are forever green
and all dwells here, held in endless peace.
Here the soul is free from the fears of darkness

and rests, held secure in this place of Truth.
All that was unclear and confused on earth
is now made clear to all.

There is no other place so full of joy
as the Pure Land of the utmost west.
Amitabha is here, clad in bright rainments
making all ready for the eternal banquet.
He draws ever troubled soul up from the earth prisons
and carries them into his peaceful Land.
The great transformation is accomplished for even the most
  lowly creature
who here is liberated from the sorrows of the body.
Here it is given a body of light
a body which shines in the sea of spirits.

Finally, there is the goddess of mercy or the bodhisattva Kuan Yin. She is held in the highest regard as one who can guide souls to the Pure Land and who in this life too will protect them. We saw earlier the description of the scale of the compassion of the bodhisattva in the *Lotus Sutra*. Here we end with a meditation on the beauty and compassion of Kuan Yin, she who will come to fetch the faithful souls and bear them away from the horrors of the Earth-prisons to the bliss of Paradise. This vision of compassionate beauty is what the believer prays to see upon death:

Her knowledge fill out the four virtues,
Her wisdom suffuses her golden body.
Her necklace is hung with pearls and precious jade,
Her bracelet is composed of jewels.
Her hair is like dark clouds wondrously coiffured like
  curling dragons,
Her embroidered girdle sways like a phoenix's wing in flight.
Sea-green jade buttons,
A gown of pure silk,
Awash with heavenly light:
Eyebrows as if crescent moons,
Eyes like stars.
A radiant jade face of divine joyfulness,
Scarlet lips, a splash of colour.

Her bottle of heavenly dew overflows,
Her willow twig rises from it in full flower.
She delivers from the eight terrors,
Saves all living beings,
For boundless is her compassion ...

She saves all the suffering when their cries reach her,
She never fails to answer their prayers,
Eternally divine and wonderful.

FESTIVALS AND SYMBOLS

BELIEFS ABOUT LIFE and death naturally find expression through festivals and art. For the vast majority of the world's population, it is these two mediums which convey the core teachings of their faith. Most of the Chinese festivals follow the lunar calendar, as opposed to the solar calendar which is used for Western dates. Use the charts in Chapter 8 to find out the corresponding Western dates up to the year 2000.

FESTIVALS

Chinese New Year

The date changes from year to year and usually falls between late January and mid-February.

The New Year is perhaps the most popular and widely celebrated traditional Chinese festival, shared with many people beyond the

Chinese community. It is believed to bring renewal and hope, and all the arguments, debts and worries of the past year must be resolved lest they influence the good luck that abounds at this time.

Six days before New Year (Day 24) a paper image of the kitchen god is burned so he can visit the Ruler of Heaven, the Jade Emperor. It is believed that during his year sitting in the kitchen this god has made a note of both thoughtful and careless acts, and once he has arrived in Heaven he will present an account of the family's deeds. In order to sweeten his report to the Jade Emperor his lips are smeared with honey. A meal is sometimes held to celebrate his departure, and the sticky rice doughnuts that are eaten then are filled with a sweet mixture as an added incentive to make a good report.

At New Year words that have associations with death, loss or bad fortune should not be uttered, fresh clothes should be worn in case bad fortune is attached to the old ones, and food is prepared which is associated with good fortune by its name, colour or shape. Meat is usually avoided as a sign of respect to animals, and oranges and tangerines often accompany the vegetable dishes since they symbolise longevity. Large balls of sweetmeats are used to predict the future. Their shapes symbolise the round of the year: if they have a smooth round shape when cooked it is a sign of good luck in the year ahead, but if they are lumpy and uneven there could be misfortune in store. Dried oysters are popular amongst traders and businessmen since the Chinese word for them sounds like 'good sales' (*ho si* in Cantonese). Fish is also eaten, since the spoken word for fish sounds like the word for 'profit' or 'surplus'. New Year cakes made specially for the festival are known as *nin ko* in Cantonese, which implies wealth and progress in the year ahead – *ko* means 'progressive' or 'high' and *nin* means 'year'. A variety of other sweet snacks are eaten to encourage good fortune and happy events.

On the day itself all work, even cooking, should be put to one side since no knives or scissors should be used and everyone takes care not to fall, tear or break anything, which is a bad omen. It is a time for visiting family and friends and a great opportunity for children to collect lucky packets of red money.

This was traditionally a time to honour the spirits, gods and ancestors – all those in the non-mortal world who might bestow blessings. Once the head of the family had offered incense and food at the house shrine, and burned paper money to help the ancestors in the next life, the doors of the house were closed to shut out restless spirits or demons wandering the streets. Firecrackers were let off to frighten away evil spirits.

Ching Ming

Moon 2 or Moon 3. This festival follows the solar calendar and usually falls on 5 or 6 April

This is a day of remembrance when the living visit their ancestors. Every member of the family has a job, whether it is preparing the food, sweeping the dust and earth away from the grave or repainting the inscriptions on the stone. When the grave is ready, incense and red candles are lit and tea, rice, vegetables, and chicken or a suckling pig are laid before the dead as offerings. Paper money or goods are burned to make sure the dead are not left without their comforts in the next life. The prayers are offered so that the spirits will rest in peace and bestow health, wealth and prosperity on the living. Before the family returns home a slip of white paper is placed under a stone on top of the grave, an indication that the grave has been visited.

Hungry Ghosts Festival

Day 15 of Moon 7

One of the most feared beings in Chinese belief is a hungry ghost. These are the spirits of those who have died but who are unable to go through the proper processes in order to be either reborn or cared for as an ancestor. There are two reasons for being a hungry ghost. First, if you commit suicide but not for honourable reasons (such as a protest against corruption in high places), you must wander this world either until your alloted time on Earth has expired and you can proceed to the Hells, or until you find another person whose body you can take over – hence the deep fear of hungry ghosts. The second reason is that you died at your alloted time but, as you had no descendants, they were unable to make the proper sacrifices and offerings – so you wander seeking someone who will. To draw attention to your plight, you cause accidents or haunt certain places or even people.

This is why each year, usually in different places each year on a ten- or twelve-year cycle, vast festivals are held. Taoist and Buddhist monks compete to liberate such souls and to make offerings to release them from their curse.

Once a year, in the seventh moon, the gates of the underworld are opened and the disillusioned and hungry ghosts come pouring out. In order to satiate them they are offered the same gifts and rites as the ancestors and Chinese opera is performed to entertain them during their wanderings.

The celebrations are usually large-scale, particularly in Hong Kong. It is an expensive operation and each region or village pays in turn. A theatre is built facing a large table bearing tall, ornate incense sticks. Behind this altar is a temporary temple which houses visiting deities. Visitors arrive night and day to pray, make offerings or watch the performances.

The festival ends with a mass offering of incence, food and paper goods. The paper objects are burned and will materialise in the spirit world, while the food is shared out amongst the visitors. While all this is happening a huge paper figure of the Jade Emperor's assistant, Tai Si Wong, is carried about. He is recording everything that happens and will report back to the Jade Emperor. There is usually a smaller figure of Kuan Yin, the goddess of mercy, standing at his side. According to one legend she was the first person to feed the hungry ghosts but they behaved so badly that she threatened to bring the King of Hell next time they were free. The ghosts were so frightened by this prospect that they have made an effort to behave ever since.

Chung Yeung

Day 9 of Moon 9 in Hong Kong, Day 1 of Moon 10 in China

The same rituals are followed as at Ching Ming, since this festival too honours the ancestors. Some families keep both festivals. As well as being a time of remembrance it is also a time for family reunion at the graveside and at home.

In Taiwan and the New Territories of Hong Kong this is the occasion for male clan members to care for the graves of their founding ancestors. The graves are cleaned and offerings are made before the men sit down to share a meal next to the spirits of the clan founders.

SYMBOLS

A number of popular symbols are associated with long life and appear on paintings, cards and statues which are given as presents and hung in the home or in temples.

Chrysanthemum This is the flower of the autumn and is particularly associated with the ninth lunar month; it is traditionally picked on the ninth day of that month. The Chinese word sounds similar to the word for 'long time' and for 'nine'. This flower is therefore associated with long life. When drawn alongside a pine tree it indicates the wish for a long and healthy life.

Cock The cock rises at dawn, the time when ghosts awake, and it is his crowing that drives them away. The cock was sometimes placed on the coffin at funeral processions because of its ability to keep ghosts at bay or to guide wandering spirits safely. Others said that the spirit of the dead was drawn into the cock when they met at the funeral and so was able to return home.

Crane One of the most popular symbols of longevity, the crane (white, yellow, blue or black) is often drawn sitting under a pine tree, also a symbol of great age. The black crane has the longest life; when it is six hundred years old it is said to refuse solid food in favour of liquids. Sometimes humans have been changed into cranes, which is why the crane expresses interest in human affairs.

Deer Since deer live many years they are associated with long life. They are the only animals said to be able to locate the rare fungus of immortality on the Earth.

Fox   The fox, familiar with the secrets of nature and ready to take on the form of a human or demon at will, is thought to have supernatural skills at its command. Since foxes were seen emerging from coffins or graves in the countryside they were thought to be the souls of the dead transmigrating to another world. To be possessed by a fox spirit is to be possessed by a dead person who wishes to return to human form, thus taking over your body.

Fungus   The ling chih is a species of fungus known as the Plant of Long Life. Such fungi were traditionally consumed by Taoists in their quest for immortality, and in its dried form it is still a symbol of longevity and eternal life. Regarded by Taoist sages as the magical fungus that grew on the mythical Isles of the Blessed in the Eastern Sea, it was said to grant eternal life to those who ate or drank it. Large specimens of ling chih were also preserved in temples or carved in gilt wood, and it often features in paintings of the Eight Immortals or Lao Tzu.

Gold   Because of gold's durability and beauty it was believed that swallowing small quantities would eventually preserve the body. Ancient emperors were fired by the claims of Taoist alchemists that they knew the secret of transmuting ordinary materials into gold.

Hare   The hare is a symbol of long life and a popular subject in Chinese art. According to one legend the hare assisted the Taoist sages by pounding the elixir of immortality. Others say that the hare lives for ever in the moon after he was willing to sacrifice his body for the Buddha.

Jade   Associated with purity, justice and intelligence, jade is believed to confer these qualities on those who wear it. Because of its hardness, weight, colour and durability it was also popular amongst alchemists and sages searching for the secret of immortality.

Owl   The call of the owl is sometimes likened to the call of death or to the voice of one spirit calling another. Some say that it sounds like the words 'dig, dig' and that just before death an owl can be heard calling, waiting to catch the soul and take it away.

Peach   The peach is the symbol of marriage, springtime and immortality. The peach of immortality was the legendary fruit of eternal life, much sought after by emperors and sages. The god of longevity (see Shou-xing) is sometimes depicted arising from a peach, and peach stones carved in the shape of locks are used as charms to protect children from death.

Pine   Because of its evergreen nature the pine is associated with long life, and since its needles do not wither in the winter it is emblematic of friends who remain constant through difficult times.

Shou-xing   This is the god of longevity who resides in the South Pole star surrounded by a garden of herbs including the herb of immortality. He often appears riding on a stag, holding the precious fruit of immortality in his hands. This life-giving peach grows on a tree that flowers once every three thousand years and only produces its fruit three thousand years after it has blossomed.

Tortoise   The meat or shell of the tortoise was a common ingredient in soups and preparations taken to prolong life. It is said that live tortoises were used as the foundation for the wooden pillars of the Temple of Heaven in the belief that they could live without sustenance for three thousand years and had the magical power to preserve wood.

White   This colour is the symbol of autumn, old age and the West. White is also associated with funerals.

THREE LIVES – PAST, PRESENT AND FUTURE

THE *THREE LIVES* is a Chinese folk classic still in use today, especially when a baby boy is born and his horoscope is made. The book catches the language and imagery of traditional Chinese folk religion and fuses together Confucian, Taoist and Buddhist elements. It consists of fifty charts and sets of predictions, and the four reproduced in this chapter are thought to reveal details of your past, present and future lives.

In the past the reading was usually given by a 'wandering' or 'wild' monk, but today it is more likely to be a Taoist monk or nun or a fortune-teller with a stall in a Buddhist temple. The reading is consulted on important occasions in the boy's life such as marriage and choosing a career. The readings were not made for girls at birth, although they could obtain one later in life.

TAKING YOUR READING

As already explained, the Western and Chinese calendars are different. Before you take a reading you will have to read Table 1 below to discover which Chinese year you were born in. First look at the left-hand column to find your year of birth. The second column indicates the date on which the Chinese New Year falls, the third the animal sign associated with that year, and the fourth the Earthly Stem (also known as Branch) associated with that year. (Earthly Stems are astrological terms which describe the divisions in the year, month, day or hour of birth.) For example, if you were born on March 18, 1960, you will find that the Chinese New Year began on January 28, your animal sign is the Rat and your Earthly Stem is Tzu. But if you were born before January 28, you will fall into the previous year and your animal sign will be the Pig and your Earthly Stem will be Hai.

The only other information you need to know is the number of your Chinese month of birth. Find the animal sign associated with your year of birth in Table 2, then find the year of your birth. The left-hand column indicates the date of the first day of each Chinese lunar month, and the right-hand column indicates its corresponding Western date. For example, if you were born on March 18, 1960 (year of the Rat) you were born in the 2nd Chinese month (which falls between February 27 and March 27).

Table 1: Chinese New Year Dates

Western year	Chinese year begins	Animal sign	Earthly stem for your year of birth	Western year	Chinese year begins	Animal sign	Earthly stem for your year of birth
1900	31 Jan	Rat	Tzu	1901	19 Feb	Ox	Ch'ou
1902	8 Feb	Tiger	Yin	1903	29 Jan	Rabbit	Map
1904	16 Feb	Dragon	Ch'en	1905	4 Feb	Snake	Szu

Western year	Chinese year begins	Animal sign	Earthly stem for your year of birth	Western year	Chinese year begins	Animal sign	Earthly stem for your year of birth
1906	25 Jan	Horse	Wu	1907	13 Feb	Ram	Wei
1908	2 Feb	Monkey	Shen	1909	22 Jan	Cock	Yu
1910	10 Feb	Dog	Hsu	1911	30 Jan	Pig	Hai
1912	18 Feb	Rat	Tzu	1913	6 Feb	Ox	Ch'ou
1914	26 Jan	Tiger	Yin	1915	14 Feb	Rabbit	Mao
1916	3 Feb	Dragon	Ch'en	1917	23 Jan	Snake	Szu
1918	11 Feb	Horse	Wu	1919	1 Feb	Ram	Wei
1920	20 Feb	Monkey	Shen	1921	8 Feb	Cock	Yu
1922	28 Jan	Dog	Hsu	1923	16 Feb	Pig	Hai
1924	5 Feb	Rat	Tzu	1925	24 Jan	Ox	Ch'ou
1926	13 Feb	Tiger	Yin	1927	2 Feb	Rabbit	Mao
1928	23 Jan	Dragon	Ch'en	1929	10 Feb	Snake	Szu
1930	30 Jan	Horse	Wu	1931	17 Feb	Ram	Wei
1932	7 Feb	Monkey	Shen	1933	26 Jan	Cock	Yu
1934	14 Feb	Dog	Hsu	1935	4 Feb	Pig	Hai
1936	24 Jan	Rat	Tzu	1937	11 Feb	Ox	Ch'ou
1938	31 Jan	Tiger	Yin	1939	19 Feb	Rabbit	Mao
1940	8 Feb	Dragon	Ch'en	1941	27 Jan	Snake	Szu
1942	18 Feb	Horse	Wu	1943	5 Feb	Ram	Wei
1944	25 Jan	Monkey	Shen	1945	13 Feb	Cock	Yu
1946	2 Feb	Dog	Hsu	1947	22 Jan	Pig	Hai
1948	10 Feb	Rat	Tzu	1949	29 Jan	Ox	Ch'ou
1950	17 Feb	Tiger	Yin	1951	6 Feb	Rabbit	Mao
1952	27 Jan	Dragon	Ch'en	1953	14 Feb	Snake	Szu
1954	3 Feb	Horse	Wu	1955	24 Jan	Ram	Wei
1956	12 Feb	Monkey	Shen	1957	31 Jan	Cock	Yu
1958	18 Feb	Dog	Hsu	1959	8 Feb	Pig	Hai
1960	28 Jan	Rat	Tzu	1961	15 Feb	Ox	Ch'ou
1962	5 Feb	Tiger	Yin	1963	25 Jan	Rabbit	Mao
1964	13 Feb	Dragon	Ch'en	1965	2 Feb	Snake	Szu
1966	21 Jan	Horse	Wu	1967	9 Feb	Ram	Wei
1968	30 Jan	Monkey	Shen	1969	17 Feb	Cock	Yu
1970	6 Feb	Dog	Hsu	1971	2 Jan	Pig	Hai
1972	15 Feb	Rat	Tzu	1973	3 Feb	Ox	Ch'ou
1974	23 Jan	Tiger	Yin	1975	11 Feb	Rabbit	Mao
1976	31 Jan	Dragon	Ch'en	1977	18 Feb	Snake	Szu
1978	7 Feb	Horse	Wu	1979	28 Jan	Ram	Wei
1980	16 Feb	Monkey	Shen	1981	5 Feb	Cock	Yu
1982	25 Jan	Dog	Hsu	1983	13 Feb	Pig	Hai
1984	2 Feb	Rat	Tzu	1985	20 Feb	Ox	Ch'ou
1986	9 Feb	Tiger	Yin	1987	29 Jan	Rabbit	Mao
1988	17 Feb	Dragon	Ch'en	1989	6 Feb	Snake	Szu
1990	27 Jan	Horse	Wu	1991	15 Feb	Ram	Wei
1992	4 Feb	Monkey	Shen	1993	23 Jan	Cock	Yu
1994	10 Feb	Dog	Hsu	1995	31 Jan	Pig	Hai
1996	19 Feb	Rat	Tzu	1997	7 Feb	Ox	Ch'ou
1998	28 Jan	Tiger	Yin	1999	16 Feb	Rabbit	Mao
2000	5 Feb	Dragon	Ch'en				

Table 2: Animal Years and Months
{ indicates double month *

Chinese	Western	Chinese	Western	Chinese	Western
•RAT		1st of 6th 18 July		1984	
		1st of 7th 17 Aug		1st of 1st 2 Feb	
1900		1st of 8th 16 Sept		1st of 2nd 3 Mar	
1st of 1st 31 Jan		1st of 9th 15 Oct		1st of 3rd 1 Apr	
1st of end 1 Mar		1st of 10th 14 Nov		1st of 4th 1 May	
1st of 3rd 31 Mar		1st of 11th 14 Dec		1st of 5th 31 May	
1st of 4th 29 Apr		1st of 12th 13 Jan 1937		1st of 6th 29 June	
1st of 5th 28 May				1st of 7th 28 July	
1st of 6th 27 June				1st of 8th 27 Aug	
1st of 7th 26 July		1948		1st of 9th 25 Sept	
{1st of 8th 25 Aug		1st of 1st 10 Feb		{1st of 10th 24 Oct	
{1st of 8th 24 Sept		1st of 2nd 11 Mar		{1st of 10th 23 Nov	
1st of 9th 23 Oct		1st of 3rd 9 Apr		1st of 11th 22 Dec	
1st of 10th 22 Nov		1st of 4th 9 May		1st of 12th 21 Jan 1985	
1st of 11th 22 Dec		1st of 5th 7 June			
1st of 12th 20 Jan 1901		1st of 6th 7 July		1996	
		1st of 7th 5 Aug		1st of 1st 19 Feb	
1912		1st of 8th 3 Sept		1st of 2nd 19 Mar	
1st of 1st 18 Feb		1st of 9th 3 Oct		1st of 3rd 18 Apr	
1st of 2nd 19 Mar		1st of 10th 1 Nov		1st of 4th 17 May	
1st of 3rd 17 Apr		1st of 11th 1 Dec		1st of 5th 16 June	
1st of 4th 17 May		1st of 12th 30 Dec		1st of 6th 16 July	
1st of 5th 15 June				1st of 7th 14 Aug	
1st of 6th 14 July				1st of 8th 13 Sept	
1st of 7th 13 Aug		1960		1st of 9th 12 Oct	
1st of 8th 11 Sept		1st of 1st 28 Jan		1st of 10th 11 Nov	
1st of 9th 10 Oct		1st of 2nd 27 Feb		1st of 11th 11 Dec	
1st of 10th 9 Nov		1st of 3rd 27 Mar		1st of 12th 9 Jan 1997	
1st of 11th 9 Dec		1st of 4th 26 Apr			
1st of 12th 7 Jan 1913		{1st of 5th 25 May		•OX	
		{1st of 6th 24 June			
1924		1st of 6th 24 July		1901	
1st of 1st 5 Feb		1st of 7th 22 Aug		1st of 1st 19 Feb	
1st of 2nd 5 Mar		1st of 8th 21 Sept		1st of 2nd 20 Mar	
1st of 3rd 4 Apr		1st of 9th 20 Oct		1st of 3rd 19 Apr	
1st of 4th 4 May		1st of 10th 19 Nov		1st of 4th 18 May	
1st of 5th 2 June		1st of 11th 18 Dec		1st of 5th 16 June	
1st of 6th 2 July		1st of 12th 17 Jan 1961		1st of 6th 16 July	
1st of 7th 1 Aug				1st of 7th 14 Aug	
1st of 8th 30 Aug				1st of 8th 13 Sept	
1st of 9th 29 Sept		1972		1st of 9th 12 Oct	
1st of 10th 28 Oct		1st of 1st 15 Feb		1st of 10th 11 Nov	
1st of 11th 27 Nov		1st of 2nd 15 Mar		1st of 11th 11 Dec	
1st of 12th 26 Dec		1st of 3rd 14 Apr		1st of 12th 10 Jan 1902	
		1st of 4th 13 May			
1936		1st of 5th 11 June		1913	
1st of 1st 24 Jan		1st of 6th 11 July		1st of 1st 6 Feb	
1st of 2nd 23 Feb		1st of 7th 9 Aug		1st of 2nd 8 Mar	
{1st of 3rd 23 Mar		1st of 8th 8 Sept		1st of 3rd 7 Apr	
{1st of 3rd 21 Apr		1st of 9th 7 Oct		1st of 4th 6 May	
1st of 4th 21 May		1st of 10th 6 Nov		1st of 5th 5 June	
1st of 5th 19 June		1st of 11th 6 Dec			
		1st of 12th 4 Jan 1973			

Chinese	Western	Chinese	Western	Chinese	Western
OX continued		**1961**		1st of 11th 30 Nov	
		1st of 1st 15 Feb		1st of 12th 30 Dec	
1st of 6th 4 July		1st of 2nd 17 Mar			
1st of 7th 2 Aug		1st of 3rd 15 Apr			
1st of 8th 1 Sept		1st of 4th 15 May		**•TIGER**	
1st of 9th 30 Sept		1st of 5th 13 June			
1st of 10th 29 Oct		1st of 6th 13 July		**1902**	
1st of 11th 28 Nov		1st of 7th 11 Aug		1st of 1st 8 Feb	
1st of 12th 27 Dec		1st of 8th 10 Sept		1st of 2nd 10 Mar	
		1st of 9th 10 Oct		1st of 3rd 8 Apr	
1925		1st of 10th 8 Nov		1st of 4th 8 May	
1st of 1st 24 Jan		1st of 11th 8 Dec		1st of 5th 6 June	
1st of 2nd 23 Feb		1st of 12th 6 Jan 1962		1st of 6th 5 July	
1st of 3rd 24 Mar				1st of 7th 4 Aug	
{ 1st of 4th 23 Apr		**1973**		1st of 8th 2 Sept	
{ 1st of 4th 22 May		1st of 1st 3 Feb		1st of 9th 2 Oct	
1st of 5th 21 June		1st of 2nd 5 Mar		1st of 10th 31 Oct	
1st of 6th 21 July		1st of 3rd 3 Apr		1st of 11th 30 Nov	
1st of 7th 19 Aug		1st of 4th 3 May		1st of 12th 30 Dec	
1st of 8th 18 Sept		1st of 5th 1 June			
1st of 9th 18 Oct		1st of 6th 30 June		**1914**	
1st of 10th 16 Nov		1st of 7th 30 July		1st of 1st 26 Jan	
1st of 11th 16 Dec		1st of 8th 28 Aug		1st of 2nd 25 Feb	
1st of 12th 14 Jan 1926		1st of 9th 26 Sept		1st of 3rd 27 Mar	
		1st of 10th 26 Oct		1st of 4th 25 Apr	
1937		1st of 11th 25 Nov		{ 1st of 5th 25 May	
1st of 1st 11 Feb		1st of 12th 24 Dec		{ 1st of 5th 23 June	
1st of 2nd 13 Mar				1st of 6th 23 July	
1st of 3rd 11 Apr		**1985**		1st of 7th 21 Aug	
1st of 4th 10 May		1st of 1st 20 Feb		1st of 8th 20 Sept	
1st of 5th 9 June		1st of 2nd 21 Mar		1st of 9th 19 Oct	
1st of 6th 8 July		1st of 3rd 20 Apr		1st of 10th 17 Nov	
1st of 7th 6 Aug		1st of 4th 20 May		1st of 11th 17 Dec	
1st of 8th 5 Sept		1st of 5th 18 June		1st of 12th 15 Jan 1915	
1st of 9th 4 Oct		1st of 6th 18 July			
1st of 10th 3 Nov		1st of 7th 16 Aug		**1926**	
1st of 11th 3 Dec		1st of 8th 15 Sept		1st of 1st 13 Feb	
1st of 12th 2 Jan 1938		1st of 9th 14 Oct		1st of 2nd 14 Mar	
		1st of 10th 12 Nov		1st of 3rd 12 Apr	
1949		1st of 11th 12 Dec		1st of 4th 12 May	
1st of 1st 29 Jan		1st of 12th 10 Jan 1986		1st of 5th 10 June	
1st of 2nd 28 Feb				1st of 6th 10 July	
1st of 3rd 29 Mar		**1997**		1st of 7th 8 Aug	
1st of 4th 28 Apr		1st of 1st 7 Feb		1st of 8th 7 Sept	
1st of 5th 28 May		1st of 2nd 9 Mar		1st of 9th 7 Oct	
1st of 6th 26 June		1st of 3rd 7 Apr		1st of 10th 5 Nov	
{ 1st of 7th 26 July		1st of 4th 7 May		1st of 11th 5 Dec	
{ 1st of 7th 24 Aug		1st of 5th 5 June		1st of 12th 4 Jan 1927	
1st of 8th 22 Sept		1st of 6th 5 July			
1st of 9th 22 Oct		1st of 7th 3 Aug		**1938**	
1st of 10th 20 Nov		1st of 8th 2 Sept		1st of 1st 31 Jan	
1st of 11th 20 Dec		1st of 9th 2 Oct		1st of 2nd 2 Mar	
1st of 12th 18 Jan 1950		1st of 10th 31 Oct		1st of 3rd 1 Apr	

*In order to keep the lunar calendar roughly in line with the western solar calendar, an extra month is added every second or third year and this is known as a double month.

Chinese	Western	Chinese	Western	Chinese	Western
TIGER continued		**1986**		1st of 10th	7 Nov
		1st of 1st	9 Feb	1st of 11th	7 Dec
1st of 4th	30 Apr	1st of 2nd	10 Mar	1st of 12th	5 Jan 1916
1st of 5th	29 May	1st of 3rd	9 Apr		
1st of 6th	28 June	1st of 4th	9 May	**1927**	
1st of 7th	27 July	1st of 5th	7 June	1st of 1st	2 Feb
1st of 7th	25 Aug	1st of 6th	7 July	1st of 2nd	4 Mar
1st of 8th	24 Sept	1st of 7th	6 Aug	1st of 3rd	2 Apr
1st of 9th	23 Oct	1st of 8th	4 Sept	1st of 4th	1 May
1st of 10th	22 Nov	1st of 9th	4 Oct	1st of 5th	31 May
1st of 11th	22 Dec	1st of 10th	2 Nov	1st of 6th	29 June
1st of 12th	20 Jan 1939	1st of 11th	2 Dec	1st of 7th	29 July
		1st of 12th	31 Dec	1st of 8th	27 Aug
				1st of 9th	26 Sept
1950		**1998**		1st of 10th	25 Oct
1st of 1st	17 Feb	1st of 1st	28 Jan	1st of 11th	24 Nov
1st of 2nd	18 Mar	1st of 2nd	27 Feb	1st of 12th	24 Dec
1st of 3rd	17 Apr	1st of 3rd	28 Mar		
1st of 4th	17 May	1st of 4th	26 Apr	**1939**	
1st of 5th	15 June	1st of 5th	26 May	1st of 1st	19 Feb
1st of 6th	15 July	1st of 5th	24 June	1st of 2nd	21 Mar
1st of 7th	14 Aug	1st of 6th	23 July	1st of 3rd	20 Apr
1st of 8th	12 Sept	1st of 7th	22 Aug	1st of 4th	19 May
1st of 9th	11 Oct	1st of 8th	21 Sept	1st of 5th	17 June
1st of 10th	10 Nov	1st of 9th	20 Oct	1st of 6th	17 July
1st of 11th	9 Dec	1st of 10th	19 Nov	1st of 7th	15 Aug
1st of 12th	8 Jan 1951	1st of 11th	19 Dec	1st of 8th	13 Sept
		1st of 12th	17 Jan 1999	1st of 9th	13 Oct
				1st of 10th	11 Nov
1962				1st of 11th	11 Dec
1st of 1st	5 Feb	**•RABBIT**		1st of 12th	9 Jan 1940
1st of 2nd	6 Mar				
1st of 3rd	5 Apr	**1903**		**1951**	
1st of 4th	4 May	1st of 1st	29 Jan	1st of 1st	6 Feb
1st of 5th	2 June	1st of 2nd	27 Feb	1st of 2nd	8 Mar
1st of 6th	2 July	1st of 3rd	29 Mar	1st of 3rd	6 Apr
1st of 7th	31 July	1st of 4th	27 Apr	1st of 4th	6 May
1st of 8th	30 Aug	1st of 5th	27 May	1st of 5th	5 June
1st of 9th	29 Sept	1st of 5th	25 June	1st of 6th	4 July
1st of 10th	28 Oct	1st of 6th	24 July	1st of 7th	3 Aug
1st of 11th	27 Nov	1st of 7th	23 Aug	1st of 8th	1 Sept
1st of 12th	27 Dec	1st of 8th	21 Sept	1st of 9th	1 Oct
		1st of 9th	20 Oct	1st of 10th	30 Oct
		1st of 10th	19 Nov	1st of 11th	29 Nov
1974		1st of 11th	19 Dec	1st of 12th	28 Dec
1st of 1st	23 Jan	1st of 12th	17 Jan 1904		
1st of 2nd	22 Feb			**1963**	
1st of 3rd	24 Mar	**1915**		1st of 1st	25 Jan
1st of 4th	22 Apr	1st of 1st	14 Feb	1st of 2nd	24 Feb
1st of 4th	22 May	1st of 2nd	16 Mar	1st of 3rd	25 Mar
1st of 5th	20 June	1st of 3rd	14 Apr	1st of 4th	24 Apr
1st of 6th	19 July	1st of 4th	14 May	1st of 4th	23 May
1st of 7th	18 Aug	1st of 5th	13 June	1st of 5th	21 June
1st of 8th	16 Sept	1st of 6th	12 July	1st of 6th	21 July
1st of 9th	15 Oct	1st of 7th	11 Aug	1st of 7th	19 Aug
1st of 10th	14 Nov	1st of 8th	9 Sept	1st of 8th	18 Sept
1st of 11th	14 Dec	1st of 9th	9 Oct	1st of 9th	17 Oct
1st of 12th	12 Jan 1975				

Chinese	Western	Chinese	Western	Chinese	Western
RABBIT continued		1st of 5th	14 June	⎧1st of 5th	24 May
		1st of 6th	13 July	⎩1st of 5th	22 June
1st of 10th	16 Nov	1st of 7th	11 Aug	1st of 6th	22 July
1st of 11th	16 Dec	1st of 8th	10 Sept	1st of 7th	20 Aug
1st of 12th	15 Jan 1964	1st of 9th	9 Oct	1st of 8th	19 Sept
		1st of 10th	7 Nov	1st of 9th	19 Oct
1975		1st of 11th	7 Dec	1st of 10th	17 Nov
1st of 1st	11 Feb	1st of 12th	6 Jan 1905	1st of 11th	17 Dec
1st of 2nd	13 Mar			1st of 12th	15 Jan 1953
1st of 3rd	12 Apr	**1916**			
1st of 4th	11 May	1st of 1st	3 Feb	**1964**	
1st of 5th	10 June	1st of 2nd	4 Mar	1st of 1st	13 Feb
1st of 6th	9 July	1st of 3rd	3 Apr	1st of 2nd	14 Mar
1st of 7th	7 Aug	1st of 4th	2 May	1st of 3rd	12 Apr
1st of 8th	6 Sept	1st of 5th	1 June	1st of 4th	12 May
1st of 9th	5 Oct	1st of 6th	30 June	1st of 5th	10 June
1st of 10th	3 Nov	1st of 7th	30 July	1st of 6th	9 July
1st of 11th	3 Dec	1st of 8th	29 Aug	1st of 7th	8 Aug
1st of 12th	1st Jan 1976	1st of 9th	27 Sept	1st of 8th	6 Sept
		1st of 10th	27 Oct	1st of 9th	6 Oct
1987		1st of 11th	25 Nov	1st of 10th	4 Nov
1st of 1st	29 Jan	1st of 12th	25 Dec	1st of 11th	4 Dec
1st of 2nd	28 Feb			1st of 12th	3 Jan 1965
1st of 3rd	29 Mar	**1928**			
1st of 4th	28 Apr	1st of 1st	23 Jan	**1976**	
1st of 5th	27 May	1st of 2nd	21 Feb	1st of 1st	31 Jan
⎧1st of 6th	26 June	1st of 2nd	22 Mar	1st of 2nd	1 Mar
⎩1st of 6th	26 July	1st of 3rd	20 Apr	1st of 3rd	31 Mar
1st of 7th	24 Aug	1st of 4th	19 May	1st of 4th	29 Apr
1st of 8th	23 Sept	1st of 5th	18 June	1st of 5th	29 May
1st of 9th	23 Oct	1st of 6th	17 July	1st of 6th	27 June
1st of 10th	21 Nov	1st of 7th	15 Aug	1st of 7th	27 July
1st of 11th	21 Dec	1st of 8th	14 Sept	⎧1st of 8th	25 Aug
1st of 12th	19 Jan 1988	1st of 9th	13 Oct	⎩1st of 8th	24 Sept
		1st of 10th	12 Nov	1st of 9th	23 Oct
1999		1st of 11th	12 Dec	1st of 10th	21 Nov
1st of 1st	16 Feb	1st of 12th	11 Jan 1929	1st of 11th	21 Dec
1st of 2nd	18 Mar			1st of 12th	19 Jan 1977
1st of 3rd	16 Apr	**1940**			
1st of 4th	15 May	1st of 1st	8 Feb	**1988**	
1st of 5th	14 June	1st of 2nd	9 Mar	1st of 1st	17 Feb
1st of 6th	13 July	1st of 3rd	8 Apr	1st of 2nd	18 Mar
1st of 7th	11 Aug	1st of 4th	7 May	1st of 3rd	16 Apr
1st of 8th	10 Sept	1st of 5th	6 June	1st of 4th	16 May
1st of 9th	9 Oct	1st of 6th	5 July	1st of 5th	14 June
1st of 10th	8 Nov	1st of 7th	4 Aug	1st of 6th	14 July
1st of 11th	8 Dec	1st of 8th	2 Sept	1st of 7th	12 Aug
1st of 12th	7 Jan 2000	1st of 9th	1 Oct	1st of 8th	11 Sept
		1st of 10th	31 Oct	1st of 9th	11 Oct
		1st of 11th	29 Nov	1st of 10th	9 Nov
•DRAGON		1st of 12th	29 Dec	1st of 11th	9 Dec
				1st of 12th	8 Jan 1989
1904		**1952**			
1st of 1st	16 Feb	1st of 1st	27 Jan	**2000**	
1st of 2nd	17 Mar	1st of 2nd	25 Feb	1st of 1st	5 Feb
1st of 3rd	16 Apr	1st of 3rd	26 Mar	1st of 2nd	6 Mar
1st of 4th	15 May	1st of 4th	24 Apr	1st of 3rd	5 Apr

Chinese	Western	Chinese	Western	Chinese	Western
DRAGON continued		**1914**		**1989**	
		1st of 1st	27 Jan	1st of 1st	6 Feb
1st of 4th	4 May	1st of 2nd	26 Feb	1st of 2nd	8 Mar
1st of 5th	2 June	1st of 3rd	28 Mar	1st of 3rd	6 Apr
1st of 6th	2 July	1st of 4th	26 Apr	1st of 4th	5 May
1st of 7th	31 July	1st of 5th	26 May	1st of 5th	4 June
1st of 8th	29 Aug	1st of 6th	25 June	1st of 6th	3 July
1st of 9th	28 Sept	1st of 6th	24 July	1st of 7th	1 Aug
1st of 10th	27 Oct	1st of 7th	23 Aug	1st of 8th	31 Aug
1st of 11th	26 Nov	1st of 8th	21 Sept	1st of 9th	30 Sept
1st of 12th	26 Dec	1st of 9th	20 Oct	1st of 10th	29 Oct
		1st of 10th	19 Nov	1st of 11th	28 Nov
		1st of 11th	18 Dec	1st of 12th	28 Dec
•SNAKE		1st of 12th	17 Jan 1942		
				•HORSE	
1905		**1953**			
1st of 1st	4 Feb	1st of 1st	14 Feb	**1906**	
1st of 2nd	6 Mar	1st of 2nd	15 Mar	1st of 1st	25 Jan
1st of 3rd	5 Apr	1st of 3rd	14 Apr	1st of 2nd	23 Feb
1st of 4th	4 May	1st of 4th	13 May	1st of 3rd	25 Mar
1st of 5th	3 June	1st of 5th	11 June	1st of 4th	24 Apr
1st of 6th	3 July	1st of 6th	11 July	1st of 4th	23 May
1st of 7th	1 Aug	1st of 7th	9 Aug	1st of 5th	22 June
1st of 8th	30 Aug	1st of 8th	8 Sept	1st of 6th	21 July
1st of 9th	29 Sept	1st of 9th	8 Oct	1st of 7th	20 Aug
1st of 10th	28 Oct	1st of 10th	7 Nov	1st of 8th	18 Sept
1st of 11th	27 Nov	1st of 11th	6 Dec	1st of 9th	18 Oct
1st of 12th	26 Dec	1st of 12th	5 Jan 1954	1st of 10th	16 Nov
				1st of 11th	16 Dec
1917		**1965**		1st of 12th	14 Jan 1907
1st of 1st	23 Jan	1st of 1st	2 Feb		
1st of 2nd	22 Feb	1st of 2nd	3 Mar	**1918**	
1st of 2nd	23 Mar	1st of 3rd	2 Apr	1st of 1st	11 Feb
1st of 3rd	21 Apr	1st of 4th	1 May	1st of 2nd	13 Mar
1st of 4th	21 May	1st of 5th	31 May	1st of 3rd	11 Apr
1st of 5th	19 June	1st of 6th	29 June	1st of 4th	10 May
1st of 6th	19 July	1st of 7th	28 July	1st of 5th	9 June
1st of 7th	18 Aug	1st of 8th	27 Aug	1st of 6th	8 July
1st of 8th	16 Sept	1st of 9th	25 Sept	1st of 7th	7 Aug
1st of 9th	16 Oct	1st of 10th	24 Oct	1st of 8th	5 Sept
1st of 10th	15 Nov	1st of 11th	23 Nov	1st of 9th	5 Oct
1st of 11th	14 Dec	1st of 12th	23 Dec	1st of 10th	4 Nov
1st of 12th	13 Jan 1918			1st of 11th	3 Dec
				1st of 12th	2 Jan 1919
1929		**1977**			
1st of 1st	10 Feb	1st of 1st	18 Feb	**1930**	
1st of 2nd	11 Mar	1st of 2nd	20 Mar	1st of 1st	30 Jan
1st of 3rd	9 Apr	1st of 3rd	18 Apr	1st of 2nd	28 Feb
1st of 4th	9 May	1st of 4th	18 May	1st of 3rd	30 Mar
1st of 5th	7 June	1st of 5th	17 June	1st of 4th	29 Apr
1st of 6th	7 July	1st of 6th	16 July	1st of 5th	28 May
1st of 7th	5 Aug	1st of 7th	15 Aug	1st of 6th	26 June
1st of 8th	3 Sept	1st of 8th	13 Sept	1st of 6th	26 July
1st of 9th	3 Oct	1st of 9th	13 Oct	1st of 7th	24 Aug
1st of 10th	1 Nov	1st of 10th	11 Nov	1st of 8th	22 Sept
1st of 11th	1 Dec	1st of 11th	11 Dec	1st of 9th	22 Oct
1st of 12th	31 Jan 1930	1st of 12th	9 Jan 1978		

Chinese	Western	Chinese	Western	Chinese	Western
HORSE continued		1st of 8th	2 Sept	1st of 4th	17 May
		1st of 9th	2 Oct	1st of 5th	16 June
1st of 10th	20 Nov	1st of 10th	1 Nov	1st of 6th	15 July
1st of 11th	20 Dec	1st of 11th	30 Nov	1st of 7th	14 Aug
1st of 12th	19 Jan 1931	1st of 12th	30 Dec	1st of 8th	12 Sept
				1st of 9th	11 Oct
1942		**1990**		1st of 10th	10 Nov
1st of 1st	15 Feb	1st of 1st	27 Jan	1st of 11th	9 Dec
1st of 2nd	17 Mar	1st of 2nd	25 Feb	1st of 12th	8 Jan 1932
1st of 3rd	15 Apr	1st of 3rd	27 Mar		
1st of 4th	15 May	1st of 4th	25 Apr	**1943**	
1st of 5th	14 June	1st of 5th	24 May	1st of 1st	5 Feb
1st of 6th	13 July	1st of 5th	23 June	1st of 2nd	6 Mar
1st of 7th	12 Aug	1st of 6th	22 July	1st of 3rd	5 Apr
1st of 8th	10 Sept	1st of 7th	20 Aug	1st of 4th	4 May
1st of 9th	10 Oct	1st of 8th	19 Sept	1st of 5th	3 June
1st of 10th	8 Nov	1st of 9th	18 Oct	1st of 6th	2 July
1st of 11th	8 Dec	1st of 10th	17 Nov	1st of 7th	1 Aug
1st of 12th	6 Jan 1943	1st of 11th	17 Dec	1st of 8th	31 Aug
		1st of 12th	16 Jan 1991	1st of 9th	29 Sept
1954				1st of 10th	29 Oct
1st of 1st	3 Feb			1st of 11th	27 Nov
1st of 2nd	5 Mar	**•RAM**		1st of 12th	27 Dec
1st of 3rd	3 Apr				
1st of 4th	3 May	**1907**		**1955**	
1st of 5th	1 June	1st of 1st	13 Feb	1st of 1st	24 Jan
1st of 6th	30 June	1st of 2nd	14 Mar	1st of 2nd	22 Feb
1st of 7th	30 July	1st of 3rd	13 Apr	1st of 3rd	24 Mar
1st of 8th	28 Aug	1st of 4th	12 May	1st of 3rd	22 Apr
1st of 9th	27 Sept	1st of 5th	11 June	1st of 4th	22 May
1st of 10th	27 Oct	1st of 6th	10 July	1st of 5th	20 June
1st of 11th	25 Nov	1st of 7th	9 Aug	1st of 6th	19 July
1st of 12th	25 Dec	1st of 8th	8 Sept	1st of 7th	18 Aug
		1st of 9th	7 Oct	1st of 8th	16 Sept
1966		1st of 10th	6 Nov	1st of 9th	16 Oct
1st of 1st	21 Jan	1st of 11th	5 Dec	1st of 10th	14 Nov
1st of 2nd	20 Feb	1st of 12th	4 Jan 1908	1st of 11th	14 Dec
1st of 3rd	22 Mar			1st of 12th	13 Jan 1956
1st of 3rd	21 Apr	**1919**			
1st of 4th	20 May	1st of 1st	1 Feb	**1967**	
1st of 5th	19 June	1st of 2nd	2 Mar	1st of 1st	9 Feb
1st of 6th	18 July	1st of 3rd	1 Apr	1st of 2nd	11 Mar
1st of 7th	16 Aug	1st of 4th	30 Apr	1st of 3rd	10 Apr
1st of 8th	15 Sept	1st of 5th	29 May	1st of 4th	9 May
1st of 9th	14 Oct	1st of 6th	28 June	1st of 5th	8 June
1st of 10th	12 Nov	1st of 7th	27 July	1st of 6th	8 July
1st of 11th	12 Dec	1st of 7th	25 Aug	1st of 7th	6 Aug
1st of 12th	11 Jan 1967	1st of 8th	24 Sept	1st of 8th	4 Sept
		1st of 9th	24 Oct	1st of 9th	4 Oct
1978		1st of 10th	22 Nov	1st of 10th	2 Nov
1st of 1st	7 Feb	1st of 11th	22 Dec	1st of 11th	2 Dec
1st of 2nd	9 Mar	1st of 12th	21 Jan 1920	1st of 12th	31 Dec
1st of 3rd	7 Apr				
1st of 4th	7 May	**1931**		**1979**	
1st of 5th	6 June	1st of 1st	17 Feb	1st of 1st	28 Jan
1st of 6th	5 July	1st of 2nd	19 Mar	1st of 2nd	27 Feb
1st of 7th	4 Aug	1st of 3rd	18 Apr	1st of 3rd	28 Mar

Chinese	Western	Chinese	Western	Chinese	Western
RAM continued		**1932**		**1980**	
		1st of 1st	6 Feb	1st of 1st	16 Feb
1st of 4th	26 Apr	1st of 2nd	7 Mar	1st of 2nd	17 Mar
1st of 5th	26 May	1st of 3rd	6 Apr	1st of 3rd	15 Apr
1st of 6th	24 June	1st of 4th	6 May	1st of 4th	14 May
1st of 6th	24 July	1st of 5th	4 June	1st of 5th	13 June
1st of 7th	23 Aug	1st of 6th	4 July	1st of 6th	12 July
1st of 8th	21 Sept	1st of 7th	2 Aug	1st of 7th	11 Aug
1st of 9th	21 Oct	1st of 8th	1 Sept	1st of 8th	9 Sept
1st of 10th	20 Nov	1st of 9th	30 Sept	1st of 9th	9 Oct
1st of 11th	19 Dec	1st of 10th	29 Oct	1st of 10th	8 Nov
1st of 12th	18 Jan 1980	1st of 11th	28 Nov	1st of 11th	7 Dec
		1st of 12th	27 Dec	1st of 12th	6 Jan 1981
1991					
1st of 1st	15 Feb	**1944**		**1992**	
1st of 2nd	16 Mar	1st of 1st	25 Jan	1st of 1st	4 Feb
1st of 3rd	15 Apr	1st of 2nd	24 Feb	1st of 2nd	4 Mar
1st of 4th	14 May	1st of 3rd	24 Mar	1st of 3rd	3 Apr
1st of 5th	12 June	1st of 4th	23 Apr	1st of 4th	3 May
1st of 6th	12 July	1st of 4th	22 May	1st of 5th	1 June
1st of 7th	10 Aug	1st of 5th	21 June	1st of 6th	30 June
1st of 8th	8 Sept	1st of 6th	20 July	1st of 7th	30 July
1st of 9th	8 Oct	1st of 7th	19 Aug	1st of 8th	28 Aug
1st of 10th	6 Nov	1st of 8th	17 Sept	1st of 9th	26 Sept
1st of 11th	6 Dec	1st of 9th	17 Oct	1st of 10th	26 Oct
1st of 12th	5 Jan 1992	1st of 10th	16 Nov	1st of 11th	24 Nov
		1st of 11th	15 Dec	1st of 12th	24 Dec
		1st of 12th	14 Jan 1945		
•MONKEY					
		1956		**•COCK**	
1908		1st of 1st	12 Feb		
1st of 1st	2 Feb	1st of 2nd	12 Mar	**1909**	
1st of 2nd	3 Mar	1st of 3rd	11 Apr	1st of 1st	22 Jan
1st of 3rd	1 Apr	1st of 4th	10 May	1st of 2nd	20 Feb
1st of 4th	30 Apr	1st of 5th	9 June	1st of 2nd	22 Mar
1st of 5th	30 May	1st of 6th	8 July	1st of 3rd	20 Apr
1st of 6th	29 June	1st of 7th	6 Aug	1st of 4th	19 May
1st of 7th	28 July	1st of 8th	5 Sept	1st of 5th	18 June
1st of 8th	27 Aug	1st of 9th	4 Oct	1st of 6th	17 July
1st of 9th	25 Sept	1st of 10th	3 Nov	1st of 7th	16 Aug
1st of 10th	25 Oct	1st of 11th	2 Dec	1st of 8th	14 Sept
1st of 11th	24 Nov	1st of 12th	1 Jan 1957	1st of 9th	14 Oct
1st of 12th	23 Dec			1st of 10th	13 Nov
		1968		1st of 11th	13 Dec
1920		1st of 1st	30 Jan	1st of 12th	11 Jan 1910
1st of 1st	20 Feb	1st of 2nd	28 Feb		
1st of 2nd	20 Mar	1st of 3rd	29 Mar	**1921**	
1st of 3rd	19 Apr	1st of 4th	27 Apr	1st of 1st	8 Feb
1st of 4th	18 May	1st of 5th	27 May	1st of 2nd	10 Mar
1st of 5th	16 June	1st of 6th	26 June	1st of 3rd	8 Apr
1st of 6th	16 July	1st of 7th	25 July	1st of 4th	8 May
1st of 7th	14 Aug	1st of 7th	24 Aug	1st of 5th	6 June
1st of 8th	12 Sept	1st of 8th	22 Sept	1st of 6th	5 July
1st of 9th	12 Oct	1st of 9th	22 Oct	1st of 7th	4 Aug
1st of 10th	10 Nov	1st of 10th	20 Nov	1st of 8th	2 Sept
1st of 11th	10 Dec	1st of 11th	20 Dec	1st of 9th	1 Oct
1st of 12th	9 Jan 1921	1st of 12th	18 Jan 1969	1st of 10th	31 Oct

Chinese	Western	Chinese	Western	Chinese	Western

COCK continued

Chinese	Western
1st of 11th	29 Nov
1st of 12th	29 Dec

1933

1st of 1st	26 Jan
1st of 2nd	24 Feb
1st of 3rd	26 Mar
1st of 4th	25 Apr
⌠1st of 5th	24 May
⌡1st of 5th	23 June
1st of 6th	22 July
1st of 7th	21 Aug
1st of 8th	20 Sept
1st of 9th	19 Oct
1st of 10th	18 Nov
1st of 11th	17 Dec
1st of 12th	15 Jan 1934

1945

1st of 1st	13 Feb
1st of 2nd	14 Mar
1st of 3rd	12 Apr
1st of 4th	12 May
1st of 5th	10 June
1st of 6th	9 July
1st of 7th	8 Aug
1st of 8th	6 Sept
1st of 9th	6 Oct
1st of 10th	5 Nov
1st of 11th	5 Dec
1st of 12th	3 Jan 1946

1957

1st of 1st	31 Jan
1st of 2nd	2 Mar
1st of 3rd	31 Mar
1st of 4th	30 Apr
1st of 5th	29 May
1st of 6th	28 June
1st of 7th	27 July
⌠1st of 8th	25 Aug
⌡1st of 8th	24 Sept
1st of 9th	23 Oct
1st of 10th	22 Nov
1st of 11th	21 Dec
1st of 12th	20 Jan 1958

1969

1st of 1st	17 Feb
1st of 2nd	18 Mar
1st of 3rd	17 Apr
1st of 4th	16 May
1st of 5th	15 June
1st of 6th	14 July
1st of 7th	13 Aug

1st of 8th	12 Sept
1st of 9th	11 Oct
1st of 10th	10 Nov
1st of 11th	9 Dec
1st of 12th	8 Jan 1970

1981

1st of 1st	5 Feb
1st of 2nd	6 Mar
1st of 3rd	5 Apr
1st of 4th	4 May
1st of 5th	2 June
1st of 6th	2 July
1st of 7th	31 July
1st of 8th	29 Aug
1st of 9th	28 Sept
1st of 10th	28 Oct
1st of 11th	26 Nov
1st of 12th	26 Dec

1993

1st of 1st	23 Jan
1st of 2nd	21 Feb
⌠1st of 3rd	23 Mar
⌡1st of 3rd	22 Apr
1st of 4th	21 May
1st of 5th	20 June
1st of 6th	19 July
1st of 7th	18 Aug
1st of 8th	16 Sept
1st of 9th	15 Oct
1st of 10th	14 Nov
1st of 11th	13 Dec
1st of 12th	12 Jan 1994

•DOG

1910

1st of 1st	10 Feb
1st of 2nd	11 Mar
1st of 3rd	10 Apr
1st of 4th	9 May
1st of 5th	7 June
1st of 6th	7 July
1st of 7th	5 Aug
1st of 8th	4 Sept
1st of 9th	3 Oct
1st of 10th	2 Nov
1st of 11th	2 Dec
1st of 12th	1 Jan 1911

1922

1st of 1st	28 Jan
1st of 2nd	27 Feb
1st of 3rd	28 Mar
1st of 4th	27 Apr

⌠1st of 5th	27 May
⌡1st of 5th	25 June
1st of 6th	24 July
1st of 7th	23 Aug
1st of 8th	21 Sept
1st of 9th	20 Oct
1st of 10th	19 Nov
1st of 11th	18 Dec
1st of 12th	17 Jan 1923

1934

1st of 1st	14 Feb
1st of 2nd	15 Mar
1st of 3rd	14 Apr
1st of 4th	13 May
1st of 5th	12 June
1st of 6th	12 July
1st of 7th	10 Aug
1st of 8th	9 Sept
1st of 9th	8 Oct
1st of 10th	7 Nov
1st of 11th	7 Dec
1st of 12th	5 Jan 1935

1946

1st of 1st	2 Feb
1st of 2nd	4 Mar
1st of 3rd	2 Apr
1st of 4th	1 May
1st of 5th	31 May
1st of 6th	29 June
1st of 7th	28 July
1st of 8th	27 Aug
1st of 9th	25 Sept
1st of 10th	25 Oct
1st of 11th	24 Nov
1st of 12th	23 Dec

1958

1st of 1st	18 Feb
1st of 2nd	20 Mar
1st of 3rd	19 Apr
1st of 4th	19 May
1st of 5th	17 June
1st of 6th	17 July
1st of 7th	15 Aug
1st of 8th	13 Sept
1st of 9th	13 Oct
1st of 10th	11 Nov
1st of 11th	11 Dec
1st of 12th	9 Jan 1959

1970

1st of 1st	6 Feb
1st of 2nd	8 Mar
1st of 3rd	6 Apr
1st of 4th	5 May

Chinese	Western	Chinese	Western	Chinese	Western
DOG continued		1st of 9th 22 Oct		1st of 5th 6 June	
		1st of 10th 21 Nov		1st of 6th 6 July	
1st of 5th 4 June		1st of 11th 20 Dec		1st of 7th 4 Aug	
1st of 6th 3 July		1st of 12th 19 Jan 1912		1st of 8th 3 Sept	
1st of 7th 2 Aug				1st of 9th 2 Oct	
1st of 8th 1 Sept		**1923**		1st of 10th 1 Nov	
1st of 9th 30 Sept		1st of 1st 16 Feb		1st of 11th 30 Nov	
1st of 10th 30 Oct		1st of 2nd 17 Mar		1st of 12th 30 Dec	
1st of 11th 29 Nov		1st of 3rd 16 Apr			
1st of 12th 28 Dec		1st of 4th 16 May		**1971**	
		1st of 5th 14 June		1st of 1st 27 Jan	
1982		1st of 6th 14 July		1st of 2nd 25 Feb	
1st of 1st 25 Jan		1st of 7th 12 Aug		1st of 3rd 27 Mar	
1st of 2nd 24 Feb		1st of 8th 11 Sept		⎰1st of 4th 25 Apr	
1st of 3rd 25 Mar		1st of 9th 10 Oct		⎱1st of 5th 24 May	
⎰1st of 4th 24 Apr		1st of 10th 8 Nov		⎱1st of 5th 23 June	
⎱1st of 4th 23 May		1st of 11th 8 Dec		1st of 6th 22 July	
1st of 5th 21 June		1st of 12th 6 Jan 1924		1st of 7th 21 Aug	
1st of 6th 21 July				1st of 8th 19 Sept	
1st of 7th 19 Aug		**1935**		1st of 9th 19 Oct	
1st of 8th 17 Sept		1st of 1st 4 Feb		1st of 10th 18 Nov	
1st of 9th 17 Oct		1st of 2nd 5 Mar		1st of 11th 18 Dec	
1st of 10th 15 Nov		1st of 3rd 3 Apr		1st of 12th 16 Jan 1972	
1st of 11th 15 Dec		1st of 4th 3 May			
1st of 12th 14 Jan 1983		1st of 5th 1 June		**1983**	
		1st of 6th 1 July		1st of 1st 13 Feb	
1994		1st of 7th 30 July		1st of 2nd 15 Mar	
1st of 1st 10 Feb		1st of 8th 29 Aug		1st of 3rd 13 Apr	
1st of 2nd 12 Mar		1st of 9th 28 Sept		1st of 4th 13 May	
1st of 3rd 11 Apr		1st of 10th 27 Oct		1st of 5th 11 June	
1st of 4th 11 May		1st of 11th 26 Nov		1st of 6th 10 July	
1st of 5th 9 June		1st of 12th 26 Dec		1st of 7th 9 Aug	
1st of 6th 9 July				1st of 8th 7 Sept	
1st of 7th 8 Aug		**1947**		1st of 9th 6 Oct	
1st of 8th 6 Sept		1st of 1st 22 Jan		1st of 10th 5 Nov	
1st of 9th 5 Oct		⎰1st of 2nd 21 Feb		1st of 11th 4 Dec	
1st of 10th 3 Nov		⎱1st of 2nd 23 Mar		1st of 12th 3 Jan 1984	
1st of 11th 2 Dec		1st of 3rd 21 Apr			
1st of 12th 1 Jan 1995		1st of 4th 20 May		**1995**	
		1st of 5th 19 June		1st of 1st 31 Jan	
		1st of 6th 18 July		1st of 2nd 1 Mar	
•PIG		1st of 7th 16 Aug		1st of 3rd 31 Mar	
		1st of 8th 15 Sept		1st of 4th 30 Apr	
1911		1st of 9th 14 Oct		1st of 5th 29 May	
1st of 1st 30 Jan		1st of 10th 13 Nov		1st of 6th 28 June	
1st of 2nd 1 Mar		1st of 11th 12 Dec		1st of 7th 27 July	
1st of 3rd 30 Mar		1st of 12th 11 Jan 1948		⎰1st of 8th 26 Aug	
1st of 4th 29 Apr				⎱1st of 8th 25 Sept	
1st of 5th 28 May		**1959**		1st of 9th 24 Oct	
⎰1st of 6th 26 June		1st of 1st 8 Feb		1st of 10th 22 Nov	
⎱1st of 6th 26 July		1st of 2nd 9 Mar		1st of 11th 22 Dec	
1st of 7th 24 Aug		1st of 3rd 8 Apr		1st of 12th 20 Jan 1996	
1st of 8th 22 Sept		1st of 4th 8 May			

YOUR PREVIOUS, PRESENT AND FUTURE LIVES

If the *Three Lives* has a core text, it is this appraisal of your most recent past life, your present and the one to come. Your conduct in one life will affect the quality of the next. Good and bad deeds will receive appropriate rewards. Happiness and prosperity in this life and in the next can best be assured by hard work and piety. This piety also ensured a better livelihood for the wandering monks who drew upon and added to this book in their role as fortune-tellers. A tight-fisted attitude towards the monks and their needs features prominently as a sure way to end up poor and unloved in the next life.

To use this section, you need your lunar month of birth (see Table 2 on p. 98). A catty is a measure of weight of approximately 1 kg. The charts in *Three Lives* are not surprisingly specific to life and conditions in China and authentic references have been retained.

First month   You were born in the first month so you were conceived in the fourth month of the previous year. In your previous life you were born in Chang Chou and your surname was Huang. You worshipped the Buddha and donated a joss-stick urn to the temple. You saved someone's life. In this life you are brilliant and physically strong. You will own land and property, but will never be able to depend on your children for financial support. You will not get on with your wife, so you will probably marry again. In your next life you will have a stable livelihood and if you are willing to work hard you are likely to achieve your goals.

Second month   You were born in the second month, so you were conceived in the fifth month of the previous year. In your previous life you were born in Nan Kuo and your surname was Chu. You were a village elder and donated a thousand scrolls (holy scriptures) to charity. In this life you have a noble and generous character. However, you will not be in harmony with your parents or brothers, and your son and daughter-in-law will prove unreliable. If you move away from your home town you will prosper. In your next life you will be successful in your career and you will enjoy a prosperous lifestyle.

Third month You were born in the third month, so you were conceived in the sixth month of the previous year. In your previous life you were born in Te Chou and your surname was Tseng. You lived in a monastery, but did not pay the fifty bowls of rice you owed as rent. You also stole clothes from an elderly person. In this life your fortune will fluctuate, but you will always have a roof over your head and enough to eat, and will keep company with the elite in both your public and personal life. You will not be able to rely on your parents or brothers. In your next life you will have many opportunities and you will need to consider your choices carefully before you act. You will have a fortunate life.

Fourth month You were born in the fourth month, so you were conceived in the seventh month of the previous year. In your previous life you were born in Szu Chou and your surname was Cheng. The malevolent fire spirit prevented you from presenting seven scrolls of T'ai Sui chanting (a traditional gift to a monastery) and you refused to guide an elderly person across a dangerous bridge. In this life you will not get on with your parents or your first wife and you will not be able to depend on your son and daughter-in-law. In spring and summer of each year you will have good fortune, but in autumn and winter your luck will be unremarkable. If you are a woman, you will never have to worry about where your next meal is coming from. In your next life you will establish good relationships with family and colleagues and will be respected by those who know you.

Fifth month You were born in the fifth month, so you were conceived in the eighth month of the previous year. In your previous life you were born in Nan Kuo and your surname was Ts'ai. You helped with the building of a Buddhist temple and gave a vegetarian meal to the monks. However, you also gave meat and strong drink to a Buddhist monk, causing him to break his dietary principles. In this life you will be wealthy and never suffer financial trouble, but you will not be able to depend on your parents, brothers, wife or children. You will live to a great age. In your next life you will enjoy a successful career and will be financially secure. You will have a dependable and trustworthy character.

Sixth month You were born in the sixth month, so you were conceived in the ninth month of the previous year. In your previous life you were born in Hua Szu Kuo and your surname was Teng. You refused to give sprays of plum blossom and ten sticks of pine to the monks. You also owed them two catties of rice and oil. In this life you will have enough to eat but never be wealthy. You will be on unpredictable terms with your parents, there will be happy times in your marriage but there will also be disruptions and you cannot always rely on relatives for support. If you are a woman, you will have minor ailments. In your next life you may have to deal with unexpected circumstances but with patience and consideration you can overcome difficulties and prosper.

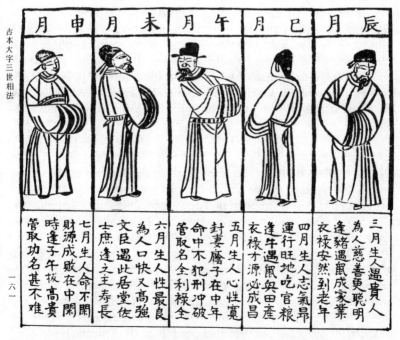

An example of one of the pages from the Three Lives.

Seventh month   You were born in the seventh month, so you were conceived in the tenth month of the previous year. In your previous life you were born in Wei Nan and your surname was Tseng. You donated a vegetarian meal to the monks, but you owed ten bolts of cloth to the monastery. In this life you will suffer hardship in your early years, but in later years you will have riches and honours. You will have many children. If you are a woman, you will have arguments with your husband and will not always be able to rely on your children. One of your sons will be skilled with his hands. In your next life your efforts will be rewarded sooner than you expect. You will have close ties with your family.

Eighth month   You were born in the eighth month, so you were conceived in the eleventh month of the previous year. In your previous life you were born in Chian Pei and your surname was Yang. You donated clothes to the monks and saved someone's life, but you also owed 156 copper coins to the monastery. In this life you will not need to worry about food and clothing. You may marry more than once and will have a small family. When you do need emotional or financial support your family may not always be able to help you. If you are a woman, you will have disagreements with your husband. In your next life you will slowly but surely build up a stable career with help from those who are close to you and will develop a reliable circle of friends.

Ninth month   You were born in the ninth month, so you were conceived in the twelfth month of the previous year. In your previous life you were born in Yung Chou and your surname was Chu. You owed the monastery two catties of oil. In this life you have an honest heart, but speak without thinking whom you may upset. You will have a roof over your head and adequate goods and clothing, but this will not always satisfy you. Your relations with your parents and brothers will be unpredictable and you will suffer from minor illnesses. In your next life your career and family prospects are good but you must not take your luck for granted. Pay attention to the people and projects which are important to you and you will be content.

Tenth month   You were born in the tenth month, so you were conceived in the first month of this year. In your previous life you were born in Huai Nan Kuo and your surname was Li. You donated ten catties of oil and fifty coins to the monastery, but you killed a child. In this life you will have a reasonable income and be an artist. Your relationship with your parents will have its share of disagreements and you will not be able to depend on your brothers. If you wish to improve your relationships, you should cultivate humility and a more yielding, giving nature. In your next life you will work in a creative field and will be respected for your skills. The efforts you make towards building up a family life and a career when you are young will eventually be rewarded.

Eleventh month   You were born in the eleventh month, so you were conceived in the second month of this year. In your previous life you were born in Sung Fo Kuo and your surname was Li. You gave a Buddhist meat and wine, breaking his vegetarian diet. In this life you will have minor heart and stomach problems but you like to drink. You will always have a roof over your head and enough to eat. There will be disagreements with your wife or your parents and your children may be unreliable. One son will be a labourer. In your next life you will have to make many decisions on your own but if you give yourself time to consider your actions they will bear fruit.

Twelfth month   You were born in the twelfth month, so you were conceived in the third month of this year. In your previous life you were born in Fu T'ai Kuo and your surname was Ch'en. You were not always honest in your dealings with other people. You had the mouth of a Buddha but a scheming nature. You also blew out the oil lights in front of the Buddha. In this life you will have a small family and be on unpredictable terms with your parents. You will work with your hands but suffer from minor ailments in your eyes, hands and feet. In your next life your fortune will be better. Do not avoid hard work because it will reap rewards for you. Your creative skills can also be put to good effect.

YOUR WEALTH FOR THIS LIFE (PURPLE MYRTLE STARS)

The names of the stars used in this section come from a system called Purple Myrtle Flower Astrology, invented in the Sung dynasty (AD 960–1279) by Chen Hsi I. The legacy from your previous life which you bring to this one is valued in terms of money and the staples of daily life. The quantities indicate how much you will enjoy this life.

To use this section, find the Earthly Stem for your year of birth in the Calendar Tables on p.96 and 97. Then find the star that corresponds to it in the chart below and look up the relevant prediction.

Earthly Stem for Year of Birth	Purple Myrtle Star
Tzu	T'an Lang
Ch'ou	Chu Men
Yin	Lu Ts'un
Mao	Wen Ch'u
Ch'en	Lien Chen
Szu	Wu Ch'u
Wu	P'o Chun
Wei	Wu Ch'u

Earthly Stem for Year of Birth	Purple Myrtle Star
Shen	Lien Chen
Yu	Wen Ch'u
Hsü	Lu Ts'un
Hai	Chu Men

T'an Lang star (Tzu)

From your previous life you have brought 130 catties of rice and 75 copper coins. You are clever but impatient. You should eat vegetarian food and be sincere and respectful to the Buddha.

Chu Men star (Ch'ou)

From your previous life you have brought 170 catties of sesame oil and 100 copper coins. You are quarrelsome and do not change your opinions easily, which could cause problems. You suffer from minor illnesses. You must set a place in your home for your ancestors.

Lu Ts'un star (Yin)

From your previous life you have brought 120 catties of rice and 50 copper coins. You are impatient and can be uncooperative. It would be a mistake for you to work away from home. You must be sincere and respectful to the god Chin Chia; then you will be protected.

Wen Ch'u star (Mao)

From your previous life you have brought 120 catties of corn and 400,000 copper coins. You are clever and will have a large fortune and prosperity in old age.

Lien Chen star (Ch'en)

From your previous life you have brought 82 catties of rice and 10 copper coins. You are thrifty with money. If you work as a civil servant you will earn a large salary. Every spring you will have good luck, but at other times you will suffer minor illnesses or injuries. If you are sincere and respective to the god Chin Chia, you will avoid evil.

Wu Ch'u star (Szu)

From your previous life you have brought 150 catties of haricot beans, 2 catties of corn and 40 copper coins. You are clever and enjoy playing games. You will study the five arts of divination and will use this knowledge in your work. You will suffer from minor illnesses. You must be sincere and respectful to the god Chin Chia so that you may have peace of mind.

P'o Chun star (Wu) From your previous life you have brought 252 catties of rice, 2 catties of haricot beans and 9 copper coins. You are kind and know influential people. You are magnanimous but will suffer from throat problems. You must be sincere and respectful to Kuan Yin, the goddess of mercy.

Wu Ch'u star (Wei) From your previous life you have brought 32 catties of wheat, 3 catties of corn and 18 copper coins. You will have periods in your life when it will be hard to earn money. You should burn incense every night.

Lien Chen star (Shen) From your previous life you have brought 502 catties of sesame oil and 10 copper coins. You are straightforward and talented. You will be able to acquire a lot of money from many sources but will have a minor accident. You should be sincere and respectful to the Buddha.

Wen Ch'u star (Yu) From your previous life you have brought 172 catties of sesame oil and 15 copper coins. You will have a fortune and need not worry about your livelihood. You must beware of a possible knife injury. You must be sincere and respectful to the Buddha.

Lu Ts'un star (Hsü) From your previous life you have brought 202 catties of rice and 82 copper coins. You are impatient, suffer from minor illnesses and would benefit from working away from home. You should be sincere and respectful to the three holy gods.

Chu Men star (Hai) From your previous life you have brought 230 catties of corn and 10 copper coins. You are proud. At first your luck will be unremarkable, but in old age you will have a good reputation and a fortune.

TRAVELLING STARS AND WEALTH STARS

There are twelve of each of these kinds of star, and your fortune at birth depends on which of them appear during the month of your birth. The Travelling Stars influence the patterns of change and stability in your life and the Wealth Stars affect your finances. In order to take a reading you need to know your lunar month of birth (see pp.98–106) and the Earthly Branch for your hour of birth. In Chinese astrology the day is broken into twelve hours, so one Chinese hour corresponds to two Western hours. In their turn the twelve Chinese hours are matched to the twelve Earthly Branches. You can find the Earthly Branch that is linked to your hour of birth in the table below. For example if you were born at 6am your Chinese hour of birth would be the 4th and your Earthly Branch, Mao.

Western hours of birth	Chinese hour of birth	Earthly branch for hour of birth
11pm – 1am	1st	Tzu
1am – 3am	2nd	Ch'ou
3am – 5am	3rd	Yin
5am – 7am	4th	Mao
7am – 9am	5th	Ch'en
9am – 11am	6th	Szu
11am – 1pm	7th	Wu
1pm – 3pm	8th	Wei
3pm – 5pm	9th	Shen
5pm – 7pm	10th	Yu
7pm – 9pm	11th	Hsü
9pm – 11pm	12th	Hai

Your Travelling Star

1. Find your Earthly Branch on the top line of the chart on p. 116.
2. Find your lunar month (discovered in Table 2) in the column below your Earthly Branch.
3. Look along the line in which your month appears, and you will find the name of your Travelling Star in the right-hand column.

Earthly Branch for Hour of Birth												Travelling Star
Hai	Hsü	Yu	Shen	Wei	Wu	Szu	Ch'en	Mao	Yin	Ch'ou	Tzu	
12th	11th	10th	9th	8th	7th	6th	5th	4th	3rd	2nd	1st	I-ma
1st	12th	11th	10th	9th	8th	7th	6th	5th	4th	3rd	2nd	Liu Hai
2nd	1st	12th	11th	10th	9th	8th	7th	6th	5th	4th	3rd	Hua Kai
3rd	2nd	1st	12th	11th	10th	9th	8th	7th	6th	5th	4th	Chieh Sha
4th	3rd	2nd	1st	12th	11th	10th	9th	8th	7th	6th	5th	Tsai Sha
5th	4th	3rd	2nd	1st	12th	11th	10th	9th	8th	7th	6th	T'ien Sha
6th	5th	4th	3rd	2nd	1st	12th	11th	10th	9th	8th	7th	Ti Sha
7th	6th	5th	4th	3rd	2nd	1st	12th	11th	10th	9th	8th	Nien Sha
8th	7th	6th	5th	4th	3rd	2nd	1st	12th	11th	10th	9th	Yueh Sha
9th	8th	7th	6th	5th	4th	3rd	2nd	1st	12th	11th	10th	Wang Shen
10th	9th	8th	7th	6th	5th	4th	3rd	2nd	1st	12th	11th	Chiang Hsing
11th	10th	9th	8th	7th	6th	5th	4th	3rd	2nd	1st	12th	P'an An
Lunar Month of Birth												

I-Ma   You will be lucky and prosperous and have a great fortune. If you are a woman you will have splendour, riches and honours. If you are a man you will own property, land and farms.

Liu Hai   You will pass through difficult times with your relatives and should learn to cultivate patience. You should spend time in a monastery and worship the Buddha.

Hua Kai   You will be lucky and prosperous. You are talented in at least three areas of the arts and will be widely respected.

Chieh Sha   Your parents may pass through periods of ill health when you are young. If you are a man you will change occupations at least three times. If you are a woman you will marry more than once.

Tsai Sha   You will encounter periods of illness and misfortune which will pass. You should pay attention to the needs of your family and not move far from them.

T'ien Sha   There will be times of upheaval in your relationship with your family. Approach business affairs cautiously and be careful of your health.

Ti Sha   You will face risks and will need the advice of older and more experienced people. You should cultivate kindness and virtue towards your family and friends.

Nien Sha You will work away from home. It will be difficult to keep regular contact with your brothers and sisters. You should always buy your own house since you are unlikely to receive an inheritance.

Yueh Sha You will have a fortune but there will not always be harmony in your marriage. Do not live in the house that you inherit – you will be luckier if you buy your own house.

Wang Shen You will move house at least three times and your most successful job will be as a government official. Your relationship with your family may sometimes be difficult.

Chiang Hsing You will be lucky and powerful. In early life you will have a great fortune, but you will be less prosperous when you are older.

P'an An You will be literary and brilliant in one of the arts. You will have a great future.

Your Wealth Star

1. Find the Earthly Branch for your hour of birth in the chart on page 115. Then locate it on the chart below.
2. Find your lunar month (Table 2) in the column below your Earthly Branch.
3. Look along the line in which your month appears, and you will find your Wealth Star in the right-hand column.

Earthly Branch for Hour of Birth												Wealth Star
Hai	Hsü	Yu	Shen	Wei	Wu	Szu	Ch'en	Mao	Yin	Ch'ou	Tzu	
2nd	1st	12th	11th	10th	9th	8th	7th	6th	5th	4th	3rd	Chien Lu
3rd	2nd	1st	12th	11th	10th	9th	8th	7th	6th	5th	4th	Ch'u Lu
4th	3rd	2nd	1st	12th	11th	10th	9th	8th	7th	6th	5th	Man Lu
5th	4th	3rd	2nd	1st	12th	11th	10th	9th	8th	7th	6th	P'ing Lu
6th	5th	4th	3rd	2nd	1st	12th	11th	10th	9th	8th	7th	Ting Lu
7th	6th	5th	4th	3rd	2nd	1st	12th	11th	10th	9th	8th	Chih Lu
8th	7th	6th	5th	4th	3rd	2nd	1st	12th	11th	10th	9th	P'o Lu
9th	8th	7th	6th	5th	4th	3rd	2nd	1st	12th	11th	10th	Wei Lu
10th	9th	8th	7th	6th	5th	4th	3rd	2nd	1st	12th	11th	Ch'eng Lu
11th	10th	9th	8th	7th	6th	5th	4th	3rd	2nd	1st	12th	Shou Lu
12th	11th	10th	9th	8th	7th	6th	5th	4th	3rd	2nd	1st	K'ai Lu
1st	12th	11th	10th	9th	8th	7th	6th	5th	4th	3rd	2nd	Pi Lu
				Lunar Month of Birth								

Chien Lu   You will have splendour, riches, honours, gold and jewellery. You will have servants and wine and meat right into old age. You will have 1000 catties of rice, 10 jars of wine each holding 18 catties, 2 catties of oil and salt, and 1000 yen.

Ch'u Lu   You will encounter financial difficulties due to a lack of inheritance, but you will have a happy and harmonious marriage. You will have 250 catties of rice, 5 catties of meat, 4 jars of wine, 1 catty and 4 taels of oil and salt, and 200 coins.

Man Lu   You will have property, land and many cattle, You will have riches and will receive help from the right person. You will have 1500 catties of rice, 12 jars of wine, 60 catties of meat, 2 catties of oil and salt, and 2000 coins.

P'ing Lu   You will be prosperous and renowned. You will have several servants, as well as 800 catties of rice, 7 jars of wine and 500 catties of meat. You will never have to worry about your livelihood. More wine and meat than you need will be provided.

Ting Lu   You will have property. You will have a harsh life in your early years, but from middle age onwards you will prosper. You are clever but impatient. You will have 10 catties of meat, 1000 catties of rice and 300 coins.

Chih Lu   Prosperity and success will be yours. After the first twenty years you will have splendour, riches and honours. You will have 500 catties of rice, 2 jars of wine, 5 catties of meat, 1 catty and 4 taels of oil and salt, and 200 coins.

P'o Lu   You will not be wealthy and will have to work hard to earn your living. Your brothers will be unable to help you and you will not receive an inheritance. You are likely to be more prosperous if you work away from your home town, and as you grow older your prosperity will increase. You will have 100 catties of rice, 1 jar of wine, 1 catty and 4 taels of meat, and 100 coins.

Wei Lu   When you are young you will suffer from minor illnesses and your brothers may not be able to help you financially, since the family property and jewellery will have been sold.

However, your children will be able to make a comfortable living. You will have 120 catties of rice, 1 jar of wine, 5 catties of meat, 10 catties of oil and salt, and 200 coins.

Ch'eng Lu   Your life will be lucky and prosperous. You will buy land, property and farms. You and your partner will always live happily. You will have 1000 catties of rice, 5 jars of wine, 12 catties of meat, 2 catties of oil and salt, and 1000 coins.

Shou Lu   You have great talent and will prosper. Your early years will be unremarkable, but later on you will be attended by good fortune. You will buy cattle and, from the age of thirty-nine or forty, will have splendour, riches and honours. You will have 1000 catties of rice, 5 jars of wine, 10 catties of meat and 1000 coins.

K'ai Lu   You will have riches and honours. You will buy property, land and farms and win fame. You will have 900 catties of rice, 1 jar of wine, 12 catties of meat and 50,000 coins.

Pi Lu   You will have a long life but will not be able to leave your children a large inheritance. You will encounter difficulties which you will eventually overcome. You will have 100 catties of rice, 3 jars of wine and 15,000 coins.

About the Editors

Martin Palmer is the director of ICOREC, the International Consultancy on Religion, Education and Culture, based in Manchester. He is a well-known authority on Chinese literature and culture, and author of books on Chinese beliefs and world religions. **Joanne O'Brien** is a member of ICOREC and the author of several books on Chinese culture and beliefs.

BIBLIOGRAPHY

The Analects (p. 21), Confucius, translated by D C Lao, Penguin, 1979

Buddhism in China (p. 12), Kenneth Ch'en, Princeton University Press, US, 1973

Chuang Tzu (p. 81), translated by Martin Palmer, Arkana/ Penguin, 1995

Doctrine of the Mean (p. 21), translated by James Legge, *The Chinese Classics*, vol 1, Oxford University Press, first published 1893

The Essential Teachings of Buddhism (pp. 49–50), edited by Kerry Brown and Joanne O'Brien, Rider, 1989

Journey to the West (pp. 59–61), translated by W J F Jenner, Foreign Languages Press, Beijing, 1982

The Lotus of the Wonderful Law (pp. 54–55), translated by W E Southill, Clarendon Press, 1930

Qigong for Health and Vitality (p. 40), Michael Tse, Piatkus Books, 1995

In Search of the Dharma (pp. 83–4), Chen-Hua, State University of New York Press, New York, US, 1992

T'ai-shangkan-ying P'ien – Lao Tzu's Treatise on the Response of the Tao (p. 58), translated by Eva Wong, HarperCollins, San Francisco, 1994

Tao Te Ching, the New Translation (pp. 78–9), Man Ho Kwok, Martin Palmer and Jay Ramsay, Element Classic Edition, 1994

Tao Te Ching (p. 9), Man Ho Kwok, Martin Palmer and Jay Ramsay, Element Books, 1994

Page references after each title entry refer to *The Book of Reincarnation and the Afterlife* not the title listed.

ALSO AVAILABLE IN THE SERIES

Lao Tzu's Tao Te Ching, a new version by Timothy Freke
Chinese Face and Hand Reading, translated by
Man-Ho Kwok and edited by Joanne O'Brien